EATING WILDLY

FORAGING FOR LIFE, LOVE AND THE PERFECT MEAL

AVA CHIN

SIMON & SCHUSTER
New York London Toronto Sydney New Delhi

90

Simon & Schuster
1230 Avenue of the Americas
New York, NY 10020

Some portions of this book have appeared, in slightly different form,
in the journal *ISLE: Interdisciplinary Studies in Literature and
Environment* and in the "Urban Forager" for the *New York Times*.
A version of the "Wild Greens Pie" recipe first appeared in
Edible Brooklyn: The Cookbook.

A few of the names in this book have been changed to protect
individual identities. However, there are no composite characters
or events in this narrative.

Please be aware that it is important to use caution when
gathering and preparing wild edibles. This book is not intended
to be a guidebook or to offer professional advice. The author and
publisher specifically disclaim all responsibility for any liability,
loss, or risk incurred as a consequence of the use of any
of the contents of this book.

First Simon & Schuster hardcover edition May 2014

SIMON & SCHUSTER and colophon are registered trademarks
of Simon & Schuster, Inc.

For information about special discounts for bulk purchases,
please contact Simon & Schuster Special Sales at
1-866-506-1949 or business@simonandschuster.com.

The Simon & Schuster Speakers Bureau can bring authors to your
live event. For more information or to book an event contact the
Simon & Schuster Speakers Bureau at 1-866-248-3049 or
visit our website at www.simonspeakers.com.

Manufactured in the United States of America

1 3 5 7 9 10 8 6 4 2

ISBN 978-1-4516-5619-0
ISBN 978-1-4516-5621-3 (ebook)

For Rose Mai, Laura J., and Mei Rose

CONTENTS

Live in each season as it passes; breathe the air, drink the drink, taste the fruit, and resign yourself to the influences of each.

—Henry David Thoreau, *Journals,* August 23, 1853

And what is a weed? A plant whose virtues have not yet been discovered.

—Ralph Waldo Emerson, *Fortune of the Republic*

The hunter or fisherman may often come home empty-handed, but the forager, though he may fail to find the particular plant he is seeking, can always load his knapsack with wholesome and palatable food.

—Euell Gibbons, *Stalking the Wild Asparagus*

Fall

1

The Search for a Wild Weed

Oyster mushrooms (*Pleurotus ostreatus*)

I am walking along a secluded, wooded path in a park in Brooklyn—my favorite place to forage for wild edibles in the city. My backpack is filled with plastic bags, a worn field edition of Euell Gibbons's *Stalking the Wild Asparagus*, and a box cutter that doubles as a knife. The wood mulch and dirt are damp beneath my sneakers as I make the slow climb up toward my destination. Down below, cyclists and joggers are making their way along the road that loops through the park, and I can hear the resounding clomp of a horse along the bridle path. In the height of early autumn, everything below is obscured by a rich tangle of leaves just starting to turn reddish gold in the morning light. A dog barks in the meadow.

I pause under the shade of a giant oak tree, scanning a fallen log where creamy white oyster mushrooms appear in the summer. We've had serious rains coupled with mild temperatures, and the air practically smells of fungi. But today, the log is bare—resembling a long, black plank under a thicket of enchanter's nightshade, with its hundreds of irksome burrs, and native pokeweed, which, while edible when young, has grown poisonous in full maturity.

This place is sacred, and not just to foragers like me. I've found the remnants of spiritual offerings in this ramble: Mardi Gras beads, a jewelry box in the shape of a grand piano, a baby cauldron tipped on its side, and even a plate of plantains, along with condom wrappers, baseballs, and empty 40-ounce bottles. More than once, I've stumbled upon the encampment of a homeless person—the plastic garbage bags, blankets, and Chinese food containers—but I've never seen anyone here except the occasional jogger, and once, a summer camp group of eight-year-olds doing a lesson on wilderness survival.

I've done this walk innumerable times, traversed over the wooded rise, across the road, and up to an even higher peak, and each time I discover something new. A chipmunk scrambling across my path before disappearing into a hollow log. An assortment of edible wild fruit—mulberries, blackberries, black raspberries—that explode with bright flavor in my mouth. A cluster of cool-to-the-touch jelly mushrooms sprouting on a decaying tree.

I forage for myself nearly every week, even in wintertime when the landscape is icy and to an untrained eye it appears that nothing is growing, but today's walk is special: I'm gathering ingredients for a pie that I'm going to enter in my first food competition. I'm on the hunt for savory lambsquarters, that free-range weed that gardeners hate but food lovers consider a culinary and nutritional treasure. Related to spinach, beets, and quinoa, Michael Pollan called lambsquarters "one of the most nutritious weeds in the world" (*In Defense of Food*). The first time I ate it raw, it fell flat on my palate—I really couldn't distinguish the edible weed from any other leafy green—but once I'd sautéed some in extra virgin olive oil with a little salt and pepper, I realized how very much it tasted like spinach. In fact, lambsquarters out-spinaches spinach in terms of pure greeny flavor.

Lambsquarters grows in backyards, on college campuses, and even around parking meters on the busiest avenues in my Park Slope neighborhood, but the best place to get it is in the park, away from traffic and pollution. It's a much-desired vegetable in Bangladeshi and Persian cuisine, but here it's considered a weed—even otherwise open-minded urban farmers I've met tend to treat it with disdain. Since lambsquarters thrives in full sunlight, I am heading toward a clearing on top of one of the highest points in Brooklyn, where the *Chenopodium album* grows on a slope unchecked, producing one of the best-tasting crops in the city.

Once on the hill, I pass a variety of familiar flora. I see the arching canes of blackberry bushes, with their smaller-than-store-bought fruit that are a lot zingier in the mouth; last month I'd picked a small container full but now the bushes are empty. Mugwort, or wild chrysanthemum, which were one-inch sprigs in spring, now brush my shoulders. In Flushing, Queens, where I was born and raised, I've encountered Chinese grandmothers collecting bundles of it for medicinal purposes—called *moxa*—where they burn the dried stalks to stop aches and pains. I bypass patches of violets with their heart-shaped leaves, so pretty in spring salads, and the insistent stalks of Asiatic dayflower, with an azure blossom that rivals the blueness of the sky, and which is as transient as your last thought.

At this peak, I sometimes encounter birdwatchers, or the occasional parks department worker wrestling weeds—the very things I like to eat—but today the peak is mine alone. Out in the distance, I can see the drape of the Verrazano, that elegant suspension bridge, which I take to my job as a professor at a local college; the giant cranes on the shoreline of Bayonne, New Jersey; and nearly everywhere I look, apartment rooftops and the verdant leafy tops of trees.

At the sunny, southern-facing slope that I like to call Lambsquarters Hill, the *Chenopodium album* are out in abundance. But instead of displaying thick goose-foot-shaped leaves, the lambsquarters have completely gone to seed: giant bunches of buds sit clustered at the top of the plant, with only the scraggliest bits of half-assed foliage below. It would take hours to collect a colander full of leaves, and even then, when cooked, it would reduce to less than a cupful of greens.

During the high, humid days of summer, I'd led a small group of newbie foragers here, and the plants were thick and lush. Picking the tops like we were snipping garden basil, we collected enough lambsquarters for a large mixed salad and a sauté with eggs for everyone. At brunch, we added to our table an assortment of wild wineberries, which many agreed tasted like a cross between a raspberry and a California orange; freshly picked Asiatic dayflower and violet leaves; some local breads and upstate cheeses; and my own homemade mulberry jam, collected from a bodacious berry-laden *Morus alba* tree only blocks away from my apartment. The others marveled at the feast, foraged mainly by their own hands, before descending hungrily into the meal.

But here I stand now, looking down at thin, paltry leaves. It's not the first time I've missed the timing of a plant, and I feel the familiar lunge of disappointment in my gut. Out of habit, I reach out and grab a lambsquarters leaf, tasting it.

It's a zero on my tongue—with a tougher consistency than

its young summertime form, and rather tasteless. When a plant diverts its energy into making seeds, it leaves the foliage with little-to-no culinary value.

I've been foraging long enough to know that what you're looking for is often elusive, and what you do find can be completely unexpected. You can train your eye, research the telltale clues and signs, but nature has a way of surprising you, especially here in the city. Even if you return to the same place, at the same time year after year, charting the weather patterns—noting the ratio of sunshine and temperature to rain—it's no guarantee that you'll get what you're looking for, no matter how well prepared you might be.

Foraging for food is a little like a mythic quest. You may think you know what you want, and expend a lot of energy and dogged determination making lists and plans for obtaining it—losing a lot of sleep and garnering no small amount of heartache along the way—only to find it shimmering elsewhere, like a golden chalice, just out of reach.

In the seasons that I've spent searching for wild edibles, taking long walks as solace after a breakup, or searching for fruit-bearing trees after the death of a loved one, I've learned that nature has a way of revealing things in its own time, providing discoveries along the way—from morel mushrooms bursting through the soil to a swarm of on-the-move bees scouting out a new home. I've been lucky enough to meet other foragers on my journey: herbalists who've introduced me to the healing properties of common weeds like motherwort and stinging nettles; Asian ladies collecting ginkgoes, those stinky fruit that litter sidewalks every fall; expert and amateur mycologists, who've taught me how to make mushroom spore prints that resemble honeycomb and starbursts, and how to cook up my fungal finds into fragrant culinary wonders; burly beekeepers who've shown me the art of relocating honeybees safely in the city and given me tastes of the sweetest wild honey. It's the unexpected bounty and regenerative powers of nature that have deepened my connection with my hometown, my family, and even myself, transforming old feelings of being "not good enough" or "unworthy" into new ways of seeing and being, like fresh wild asparagus or violets erupting from the earth every spring.

But this morning, I make my way down the hill empty-handed. Lambsquarters is one of the most sustainable, abundant foods available here, and without a big bagful of it, I am in serious trouble for this food competition. It doesn't help that we are in between seasons: all the summer berries have disappeared—even the elderberry peaked early, so that only a few clusters remain on the trees—and it's too soon for the new dandelion and garlic mustard rosettes to appear.

Ordinarily, I go home through a shortcut on the road, my bag filled with goodies, but today, I double back to the old path that led me here.

Back under the shade of tall trees, I pass a fallen log lying horizontally alongside the path. This is where the reishi mushrooms grow—a medicinal fungus that boosts immunity and is prized in Chinese medicine. Even though *Ganoderma lucidum* cannot help me with my dish, out of habit I peer over the log, which is damp and coming apart under the weight of my fingers. But there is only the ribbonlike curl of a few turkey tail mushrooms clinging to the bark.

I straighten up, disappointed, when there it is: that smell of mushrooms in the air again, and it's not coming just from those turkey tails. Usually, I scan the ground for fungi hidden in the decaying wood or growing on piles of mulch or dead leaves, but this time my eye goes up an old tree—a tree with dark, grooved bark that's nestled so closely among its neighbors that it's grown its branches up high in order to reach the sun. It is impressive: stories tall, higher than my fourth-floor walkup apartment. I cannot make out what kind of tree it is from its faraway leaves. But then right where the trunk ends and the first of many central branches begin, I see it: a wide, creamy white cluster of oyster mushrooms spreading out from the tree like Chinese fans.

I peer up under it as close as I can manage. The mushrooms are a light beige-cream color, with barely a tint of yellow on the edges, and very young and fresh. The delicate gills run down the short, almost nonexistent stem. Although you really need to make a print of the mushroom spores—the cells that allow fungi to replicate and grow—to make a proper identification, I know that if I had microscopic vision, I'd be able to see the white spores gently raining down. A mushroom—the fruiting body of a network of threadlike mycelium that thrives underground or inside decaying wood—is the organism's virulent attempt to reproduce. This act of self-propagation, prompted by the right timing of weather conditions and moisture, is what I, and other foragers and mushroom-hunters like me, see as a supreme eating opportunity.

I'm on my tiptoes trying to reach the mushrooms, but all I feel is the rough bark under my fingers. I jump up and miss them entirely. Tree-climbing was a favorite activity when I was a kid, but when I try to scale the trunk, my sneakers slide off the surface as if it's been waxed.

Across the leafy ground, I spy a log the size of a small wastepaper basket several yards away. It's too heavy for me to lift and carry, but after a few moments of pushing, tugging, and kicking, I discover that I can roll it with both hands until it sits at the base of the tree.

I climb aboard the log, which wobbles under my weight, and now I can just about grab hold of the entire cluster of oysters. I rip a section off with my fingers—separating the flesh from the bark of the tree, my chin pressed up against the trunk. I am so focused on getting this lovely hunk of *Pleurotus ostreatus* that I forget about the blade in my knapsack or the precariousness of my footing. All of my tugging and pulling disturbs a spider the size of a quarter, which races out of the mushroom's white folds. I laugh as it crawls on delicate, spindly legs across my fingers, tickling me, and disappears into a peel of bark.

I step off the log with over two pounds of oyster mushrooms heavy in my hands.

2

Flushing, Queens, 1970s

Cloud ear (*Auricularia auricula, A. polytricha*)

When I was a kid, there wasn't anything I liked better than to sit in the mostly concrete courtyard of my mother's apartment building, digging into the loamy soil with a spoon. Digging revealed a truth that never ceased to amaze me—that the earth was rich in hidden wonders, a veritable storehouse of free goodies: fat, writhing worms; old, tarnished coins; gnarled roots like my grandmother's arthritic hands. I sometimes sat there for hours, surrounded by elderly neighbors who just shrugged when they saw me, the only grade-schooler in the building, with dirty hands and knees, searching for natural treasures.

One day, I disappeared behind the hedges under the shadow of sycamore trees, my mother talking to a neighbor only a few yards away, her booming laughter and teacher's voice becoming more distant as I edged around in the shade. It had rained the day before and the earth smelled dark and rich, almost like chocolate. I had distinguished from the blades of grass something taller, more fragrant, wilder—something that resembled green grass gone haywire, like a mad professor's hair.

When I grabbed the mass of it in both hands and pulled with all my strength and weight, my forearms and thighs straining, the plant came up—bulbs and all—and I was hit by flying soil and the pungent smell of scallions, reminiscent of the kind my grandfather used in my favorite lobster Cantonese dish, which he made every Chinese New Year and on my birthday.

I couldn't have been happier. I had no idea what the plant was called, but I knew it was edible. Even when my mother yelled, "Put that down!" I was unable to stop marveling at the long chivelike leaves and the oniony scent.

While her back was turned, I snuck back into the hedges and ate it. The green stalks were both sweet and bitter, an intense blend of scallions and garlic.

My grandfather, a former Toisanese village boy turned Chinese restaurant worker, taught me how to eat. Grandpa spoke an English so informed by the cadence of his native dialect that he didn't talk so much as bark, so that he often sounded like he was yelling from across a muddy field rather than just across the kitchen table. He had learned to sauté, braise, and sear from the cooks at the various Manhattan restaurants in which he worked. His palate was so diversified that he could make almost anything well. Sometimes it was a whole fish from head to tail—first steamed, then drizzled with a piping-hot medley of ginger, scallions, garlic, and sesame oil. Soy sauce chicken wings dripping in a brown sugar glaze. American fried chicken dipped in a garlic-ginger batter that had my friends sighing with delight—even the ones with hard-core Southern roots often asked for seconds.

By four years old, I was already cracking open crabs with a nutcracker and devouring lobsters from claw to tail. Even the legs, those tiny crawlers that are often tossed aside for being too slim pickings, revealed a sweet juice as I gnawed on them like teething rings. I learned to eat snails in black bean sauce by teasing them out of their shells with a toothpick—the meat emerging like a coil of dark pasta. (My favorite part, aside from the succulent, silt-colored briny snail, was the little door the size of my pinkie fingernail.) Members of my family claim that I ate anything my grandfather fed me, including fish eyeballs, which I later vehemently denied, although I do have a vague memory of eating something round and gelatinous, with a texture like vanilla pudding.

My grandparents' home, where my mother often dropped me off on Friday afternoons before her dates, was always filled with the sounds and smells of good food. Late at night, I would often climb out of my grandmother's queen-size bed in a half-daze, awoken by the *zing!* of Grandpa sharpening his cleaver before pounding the chopping block. I'd plop myself down at the kitchen table where my grandfather, home from closing the restaurant, would share his meals with me: a slab of perfectly seared liver just out of the pan, or sizzling flash-fried bok choy with shiitakes.

Saturday mornings, the house would be filled with the smell of sautéed garlic, and before I even entered the kitchen, I was salivating, knowing that something good—a slow-cooked tomato sauce, or a Chinese winter melon soup—was simmering on the stove. My grandfather started cooking dinner early in the morning so it would be ready to set down at six o'clock, which also conveniently allowed him to slip away to the race-track for a few hours while everything was percolating.

Even though dinner would often be only my grandparents and myself—my extended family lived miles away in different parts of suburban Long Island—every weekend was an excuse for an elaborate feast. Lobster Cantonese with fresh scallions covered in lacy egg whites and ground pork. Velvety corn soup with thin-sliced pork and minced onions.

I always sat between my grandparents, the welcome recipient of giant spoonsful of food landing on my plate from either direction. Sometimes my mother joined us, as my grandparents heaped hunks of de-shelled lobster or crabmeat in front of me. When she was there, my mother regarded the parade of delicacies surrounding me like a jealous older sister—she'd grown up the baby girl under two older brothers, and disliked my usurping her role in the family—but mostly, my mother was out on dates, trying to find a good-enough man who wouldn't walk away.

A stunner as a newborn ("Even on the bus, everyone wanted to hold her," my grandmother liked to recount), my mother had the pick of the litter when she bloomed onto the 1960s Chinese American dating scene, wearing handmade taffeta dresses fitted with modest necklines and full, poofy skirts. She had the kind of wide-eyed, apple-cheeked, bee-stung-lips type of beauty that attracted men in droves.

By the time she was crowned Miss Chinatown in her early twenties, my mother had taken up with my father, an extremely charming lawyer and divorced dad who was running for State Assembly. Stanley was closer to my grandparents' age than to hers, and my grandfather, a bit of a former playboy himself, recognized him as an entitled member of the club. "That guy—" my grandfather would always say, shaking his head and never finishing the sentence, instead throwing more salt or scallions into whatever pot or pan he was standing over.

My father left us when my mom was pregnant with me, and we never saw him again, except for the times she took him to court for child support. We lived with my grandparents until I was two, before my mother's brief marriage to my stepfather. After that came the Era of the Boyfriends. Like my father and stepfather, these men were tall and good-looking, guys who stood out from the crowds at bars and nightclubs.

"I want to find a daddy for you," she sometimes said, and for a while, when I was very young, I tried to win them over, too. Sometimes I stretched an old, oversized sweater over my knees and mimicked the noises and movements of an owl, cooing "Who?" to the hoots and howls of my mother and her latest boyfriend as they drank vodka cocktails on the couch. I waved my report cards under their noses, or showed off my art projects, dropping a trail of gold glitter on the floor.

But as the years went by, I eventually grew a thick skin to my mother's love life, thankful it left me in the weekend company of my grandparents and copious amounts of food.

"What's this called?" I asked one evening at the kitchen table, when a platter of beef and Chinese broccoli—plus a mysterious dark ingredient that resembled a squiggly mass of seaweed—was placed before me.

"*Choy sum ngàuh yuk,*" my grandmother said, pushing her chair up toward the table.

"No," I said, picking out the brown object the size of a dime with my chopsticks, "*this.*"

"It's a cloud ear fungus," my grandmother said. "*Wun yee.* Sometimes called tree ear." Then, pointing with a bony finger that was becoming more and more arthritic with age, "See the shape?"

"Does it grow in the woods or the sea?" I asked, sniffing it. It only smelled like my grandfather's dark, savory sauce.

"Eat!" Grandpa ordered in his deeply resonant voice, placing individual bowls of rice down on the table. He put a heaping spoonful of food onto mine, making an indent into my mound of *fan* with the back of the serving spoon so the cloud ear wouldn't fall off. "It'll make you beautiful."

In our family, beauty was an asset, even above my grandmother's keen intelligence and my mother's degrees. ("Men don't make passes at girls who wear glasses," said my wire-framed-glasses-wearing grandmother, who loved quoting Dorothy Parker.) If all it took to look like my mother instead of my good-for-nothing father was eating an unusual-looking fungus, then I wanted in. I quickly dug into my food.

The cloud ear was cool and malleable—similar to abalone or jellyfish—but like the way a good diamond had clarity and was colorless, on its own the *wun yee* was mild and flavorless. Mostly, I liked the crunch.

Every meal after that, whenever *wun yee* was served, I made certain to eat it. Whenever my cousins came over for dinner, I even ate their leftovers.

One summer, my day camp took us out on a fishing boat, where we spent hours off the coasts of Brooklyn and New Jersey angling for striped bass and fluke. I caught nothing all morning except winged sea robins that barked as I tossed them back into the water. But just before we headed back to shore, something large and heavy tugged on my line. I quickly reeled it in. After a few heart-thumping moments, a glistening fluke emerged, flapping in the afternoon light, spraying me and my fellow campers with salt water. It was large enough to keep.

I brought my fish home to my grandparents, who made a big fuss after unwrapping it in the kitchen.

Instead of preparing it the Chinese way—the whole fish from head to tail, steamed, then sautéed in hot oil and aromatics—my grandfather covered it in batter and dunked it in the fryer. Ten minutes later, it appeared on our table, a fillet of fluke, with a side of ketchup.

At first, I was disappointed. It looked so tiny on the plate, like a perfect square of fried cheese.

But as we sat there surrounding the plate, digging into its white flakey goodness with our chopsticks, the fish melting in my mouth and combining with the crunchiness of my grandfather's batter, I felt like I was tasting a bit of heaven.

Here was a fluke that I'd caught with my own hands, off the cold, icy waters of the city. The ocean, like the soil, was alive with goodies, and at that moment, watching my grandparents digging into the small fillet, which was disappearing before my very eyes, I felt something akin to pride.

When I wasn't busy devouring their food, I often tagged along with my grandparents down the aisles of Chinese supermarkets. While Grandma stuck to purchasing standard items like saltines or milk to add to her morning coffee, Grandpa knew the secrets of the dried, preserved goods and vegetables tucked away in the stores' dusty corners.

The darker, more foresty-smelling mushrooms (*dong gu*), which were collected in bins and cost five times more than the packets of fungi that packed the aisles, were worth the price for their better flavor and immunity-boosting properties; the glass jars of loose green teas were good for keeping one mentally sharp, whereas the red teas were renowned for aiding digestion, which is why we drank them by the teapot-full with dim sum; dried chrysanthemum blossoms were good for headaches; the red hawthorn berries, which were pressed into the candies I adored sucking on, were beneficial for the heart; and then there were the giant jars of pungent *dong quai*—the "female ginseng"—which lined the medicine shelves like pieces of twisted ivory and were beneficial for when I became *a woman*.

I'm not sure how Grandpa knew what he knew—whether his parents had taught him or he'd learned from the cooks at the restaurant—but I just chalked it up to his being more inherently Chinese than I was and that somehow the knowledge came with the territory.

One day, I watched my grandfather sifting through one of the giant bins of mushrooms at the front of the store. "What's that?" I asked, peering into the waist-high container.

"*Dong gu,*" he said, sifting through the dark dried shiitakes. "The thick ones are good, with the cracked tops. Smell. *Good.*" I leaned over his hands and inhaled. They were earthy and deeply fragrant.

I followed my grandfather over to another bin.

"*Wun yee,*" he said, pulling out a few dark squiggly bits. "Cloud ear."

The cloud ears were hard and velvety and looked like Shrinky Dinks after being pulled out of the oven. One side was silvery white, the other the color of black ink. I wasn't expecting this: in our stir-fries they were always soft, and almost translucent—and when held up to the light, a deep amber.

So that's what they look like, I thought, staring at the bin full of fungi, with its handwritten *$20/lb.* sign written in Magic Marker.

On weekends, I searched our apartment the same way that I dug into the earth, looking for clues of my father. Among the books, the magazines, and the antique vases and ashtrays my mother collected throughout the years, these were the things he left behind: a stuffed koala bear he'd given to my mother early on in their courtship, which I slept with and drooled on at night, clutching its matted fur and plastic paws. A sexy diamond-cut engagement ring that I saw in my mother's jewelry box once, before she hawked it to pay our rent. A tiny and unembellished gold infant cross, which had been sent along by my paternal grandmother, whom I'd never met.

The only photograph of him that we had was a $3\frac{1}{2}$-by-$3\frac{1}{2}$-inch color square taken with an old Brownie camera. My mother showed it to me one evening while we were sitting around the living room watching the six o'clock news.

Mom was tense—for the past week, her full mouth had been drawn into a line so tight it appeared as if rendered by an artist's brush, and the stereo from which she enjoyed blasting R&B music was silent. She stomped around the apartment slamming objects and burning nearly every meal. I wasn't sure why she was so upset until I overheard her complaining to a friend on the phone that my father owed back payments on child support.

"This is your father," she said, her normally rich voice sounding low and clipped.

In the photograph, Stanley was lean and handsome, sitting with his legs crossed on my grandparents' recliner. The camera had caught him relaxed and mid-laugh, his arms spread out onto the chair rests. While growing up, I'd heard the rumors that we looked alike, and it was true: we had the same-shaped face and maple-syrup eye color, and if I looked at the picture from out of the corner of my vision, I might have thought I was looking at an older version of myself.

I reached for the photo, but Mom was quicker.

"Take a good look," she said, holding the picture over a ceramic ashtray before striking a tall kitchen match with her long, thin fingers. Her hands were shaking—whether it was from nerves or excitement, I couldn't tell—but the perfect ovals of her fingernails were illuminated when the match finally lit.

Before I could protest, the photograph caught fire—first crinkling up around the edges, before the whole picture warped and shrank in the turbulence of the flame. Mom's eyes were glowing, reflecting the reddish-orange light, and her mouth was back to its satisfied pout, though tension still lingered around the edges. The flame consumed the paper in seconds, until it came dangerously close to her fingers. She dropped it into the ashtray, and we watched the entire image of my father dissolve into a hot curl of smoke.

"That's that," she said, wiping her hands against each other, as if wiping them clean of the whole affair.

⁓

"What was he like?" I asked my grandmother one evening as I was pinning up her hair into rollers. Grandma was the only one in the family who would talk to me about my father.

"He was tall and good-looking," Grandma said, watching the end of her favorite television program. "He comes from a big family—too bad they don't look you up."

As an only child, I longed for a big family, and tried to envision what it would be like to be part of a big clan.

"Your mother was young and beautiful. She was never the same after what your father did to her," Grandma said, as the credits rolled across her glasses. "He used her and then threw her away." Then, sighing, "Oh well, what can you do?"

I always wanted to cry after these conversations, where I felt the mix of sadness and guilt settle in my stomach like the glasses of Scotch and watery ice my grandfather poured for himself at the end of every workweek. Instead, I rooted around the bottom of the curler box.

Winter

3

Into the Urban Wild

Field garlic (*Allium vineale*)

I t was a frigidly cold February morning in Brooklyn, as I climbed the winding footpaths of Fort Greene Park with my friend and foraging partner, Eli. I was on my first assignment for an online section of *The New York Times*, writing for my new, still unnamed column for an editor whose work I'd long admired. This new foraging column, if I could pull it off, would ensure my landing tenure at my day job as a writing professor at a local college. Without it, I could kiss my job good-bye.

I had been foraging for only a few months when I met Eli last fall on a foraging tour of Prospect Park with the "Wildman" Steve Brill. Being professors of around the same age (in his case, a former professor turned green architect), we became on-the-spot fast friends, discussing life, love, and the craziness of academia while gathering rangy hedge mustard, tart carnelian cherries, and tennis-ball-size black walnuts. We were both nursing broken hearts: I'd parted with my boyfriend, Robert, a Southerner who enjoyed swing dancing, whom I had long dreamed of marrying; Eli was splitting with his girlfriend of six years, a woman so insecure that she'd once been jealous of his relationship with a neighbor's dog.

Eli and I bonded while digging up wild parsnips and burdock roots, which frustratingly broke under our trowels. While I was good at finding the vegetables hidden among the autumn foliage, Eli proved to be a patient and diligent digger, able to excavate taproots as long as his forearm. On days that I wasn't teaching and Eli didn't need to log in hours with the telecommuting job he had at an architecture firm in Boulder, Colorado, we spent hours foraging together in the rain and near-freezing temperatures.

Our breath fanned out before us in little clouds, and I dug my gloved fists deeper into my coat pockets. For the past few weeks, the morning temperatures had barely risen above freezing, and as Eli and I walked across the stark brown landscape, the bare trees skeletal against the gray sky, only the persistent pines were thick with lush, needlelike leaves. We were still in the dormant period, when other foragers hung up their cloth bags, relying on stockpiles of wild berry preserves, dried mushrooms, and dreams of springtime foraging to get them through the winter. Only I was foolish enough to believe that I could find anything edible this time of year. As we continued along the footpath, we were surrounded by dead leaves and compacted earth. My heart sank.

"I'm doomed," I said, as the wind suddenly picked up. I tucked my wool hat below the tips of my ears. "Better tell my editor I quit before he gets his hopes up."

"C'mon," Eli said, walking a little faster. Even though it was late morning, he was already sporting a stubbly, reddish-blond five-o'clock shadow. "We just got here."

Even in good weather, Fort Greene, Brooklyn, and adjacent Clinton Hill—the areas that my new column covered—wouldn't be anyone's idea of prime foraging terrain. These were beautiful, historic, largely middle-class black neighborhoods filled with Victorian brownstones, where writers and artists had established a thriving arts scene. Film director Spike Lee's production company 40 Acres and a Mule was located on the same block where activist friends lived—backyard-composting fifteen years before it became fashionable around the city.

The neighborhood park we were traversing was a hilly urban oasis complete with tennis courts and views of Manhattan. In addition to being Brooklyn's first park, it was the site of a Revolutionary War fort, and was flanked by a mix of hospital buildings, brownstones, and low-income housing projects. It was heavily used by joggers, dog-walkers, and neighborhood kids, but contained none of the more secluded, woody areas that I was used to nosing around in for my meals.

What I didn't tell Eli, although I suspect he already knew it, was that I was afraid. Scared shitless.

The night before, I had written down a list of my worst fears. These included:

1. Readers were going to see right through me and suspect that I was a fraud. I hadn't been foraging all that long, so why should they trust me?
2. I held multiple advanced degrees in English, not botany. This was only a hobby, albeit a fascinating one, so what the hell did I know about the taxonomy of wild urban plants?

3. Readers were going to think I was a crazy person for eating things off city streets. (And perhaps they were right—even to me, foraging in the city did seem a little strange.)

4. Residents were going to assume I was plundering and harming the neighborhood flora. How was I going to convince them that I *loved* the local flora?

The first few fears were surprisingly similar to those I had when I first started teaching. Although I had a passion for it, in those early days I was terrified that my students would think, "She doesn't know what she's talking about."

Even I had to admit that foraging in the city's green spaces was a little, er, unusual. The practices of a mad, wild woman. The image of the forager was typified by the "Wildman" Steve Brill himself—a crunchy-granola hippie type who wore socks over his trousers and neglected to trim his beard. I struggled to see where I fit into that paradigm.

Although Eli and I had stopped going on Brill's tours months ago, we still invoked him fondly: "Steve said this was good for _____," or "Remember when we found this with Steve?" Brill, who then called himself "America's Best-Known Forager," was prone to Borscht Belt humor and using his mouth like a performance kazoo, sometimes belting out Chopin's "Funeral March" to underscore the deadliness of a certain plant. Whenever anyone asked him about the legalities of foraging in city parks, he would promptly launch into the story of how he'd once been arrested for eating a dandelion in the 1980s—and then how the Parks Department dropped the charges and eventually hired him to lead tours.

But even Brill wasn't crazy enough to run foraging walks

in Fort Greene, preferring to stick to the larger, more densely wooded Central and Prospect parks.

As we headed uphill, surrounded by nothing but brittle foliage and straw-colored grass, where even the sturdy ginkgoes had long since shed their leaves and malodorous fruit, I slowly came to realize like a weight settling in my stomach just how much trouble I was in attempting to do the impossible. Unfortunately, it was an all-too-familiar feeling.

When I was in college, my writing professor said that my father was the wound that made me a writer. Back then, I wasn't focused on the natural world—instead, I was constantly writing fiction and plays about daughters reconciling with long-lost fathers, and single mothers in turmoil. In my twenties, while working for national newspapers and magazines covering music and the arts, I secretly believed that actually finding my father would be the answer to all of my problems, and when I was twenty-six years old, we finally met.

Stanley was a tall, handsome, and semiretired Chinatown lawyer who, at seventy-three, had been married and divorced five times, twice to the same woman. He had a charming, effortless manner that was only undermined by a slight bodily quivering that I suspected wasn't nervousness or caffeine withdrawal, but the cumulative effect of doing too many drugs in the carefree 1970s.

Although it was wonderful to see where I had come from— we had the same manner of walking and talking and even vaguely the same fashion sense—after a glorious year of getting to know him, my father soon reverted to that Houdini-like state of now-you-see-me-now-you-don't with which he was so comfortable.

One day, on the busy streets of Chinatown, just before I moved away to attend graduate school, I confronted him.

"Where've you been? I've been trying to reach you for over a month," I said, my voice rising an octave as it always did whenever I was about to lose control. We were standing on the corner of Canal and Centre streets, and I didn't care if anyone else heard me. "I sent you letters—left messages on your machine."

"Why did you get in touch if all you wanted to do is be mad?" my father said, looking a little frightened and trying to edge away. He stepped out suddenly into oncoming traffic and was nearly hit by a speeding taxicab.

"I have the right to be angry," I said, grabbing him back and nearly shaking him. I could almost feel his bones through his shirtsleeve. We both knew that I was referring to more than just this last month. "I'm your daughter—stop trying to run away from me!"

"What about me?" he said, his voice sounding suddenly desperate. "Why doesn't anyone care about what's going on with *me*?" Family members were angry because he'd decided to live with his girlfriend, a singer with a cocaine habit.

"This isn't about you!" I yelled. Despite the fact that he seemed to be shrinking in front of my eyes, I was too angry to care. I was sick and tired of being overlooked. "I've been trying to get ahold of you and you've just been ignoring me. Do you have any idea how that makes me feel?"

We stood there for several moments, not saying anything. All around us, vendors were busy selling knockoff designer perfume and handbags. A worker outside a fish market sprayed down the street with a hose. We were surrounded by traffic, as cars coming off the bridge barreled their way across the island toward the tunnel.

Although it felt good to finally voice my anger, and he sent a card later that week asking my "forbearance," the only thing that changed in that moment was the traffic light, as dozens of pedestrians from both sides of Canal rushed out onto the crosswalk and flooded the street corners.

As Eli and I continued our search for wild edibles throughout Fort Greene Park, the taste of disappointment was heavy in my mouth. We'd nearly come full circle without finding anything, and I could already feel the flutter of anxiety start to kick in as I considered the possibility of not being able to fulfill my duties to my new editor. Unlike in college or during my twenties, so much of my writing now was dependent upon what was happening in nature and the environment, and most of it was entirely beyond my control. My knapsack was stuffed with plastic bags ready for filling, but as my eye followed the path up the hill and down toward the conifers, all I could see was a bare landscape empty of any vegetation.

"Let's try up there," I said, pointing a gloved hand toward the empty tennis courts. "Maybe there'll be something growing along the fence."

The hill was covered in matted leaves and grass, and icy patches that cracked under our boots. Spring was still several weeks away, and it would be awhile before we'd start to see the first green shoots pushing through the earth. As we climbed toward the tennis courts, a garbage bag caught in the chain-link fence blew noisily in the wind like a downed kite. Out of the corner of my eye, I noticed a dense row of brown bramble several yards away—old rosebushes, prickly and skeletal without their leaves. I slowed down, and as my vision started to sharpen, I spied something greenish growing low among the branches.

Eli followed me down the hill, where I slid a little on curled and brittle leaves, despite my lugged boots, before gaining traction at the foot of the bushes. Parts of the bramble were shoulder height; others towered over me like a thorn forest in a fairy tale. But there, under the spiny branches and woody stems, was a patch of mature field garlic that had survived the winter—scraggly, bent over, yet verdant above the dead, matted grass.

"Look at that," I said, pulling off my gloves.

I tore off a small strand and the plant released its oniony scent into the air. I held it out to Eli, who sniffed it. "Wow," he said, pulling back and quickly taking out his camera.

As I chewed, the tangy garlicky flavor flooded my mouth. I was salivating the way I used to as a kid pulling it up from the backyard, long before I ever went out on a tour with Steve Brill and learned its name.

"*Field garlic*," I murmured as Eli snapped a picture.

Field garlic (*Allium vineale*), aka wild onion or wild garlic, resembles a cross between scallions and chives, but with a more severe flavor and oniony fragrance. With long green shoots and whitish bulbs, it proliferates in more than half the states in the country (mostly parts of the Midwest and throughout the East); in some places, including California, Arkansas, and Hawaii, it is listed as a noxious weed. A European native, cows enjoy eating its springtime shoots, which can negatively affect the flavor of their milk.

According to Euell Gibbons, 1960s foraging guru and author of *Stalking the Wild Asparagus*—my forager's bible, which I read and reread throughout the long winter evenings—there were no poisonous species of wild onion, although some were better-tasting than others. (Gibbons himself preferred meadow garlic [*Allium canadense*] and wild leeks [*Allium tricoccum*] to field garlic.)

I posed with the plant, which was starting to feel like an old friend, framing it with my reddening hands, before snipping off a few strands. Younger spring *Allium* was best for salads, but this batch would be fine in soups or lightly sautéed as a substitute for scallions. Since the plant propagated through its white bulbs, we left the rest alone to soak in the rays of the wintry sun.

As we nosed farther along the edges of the bramble, I found the toothed leaves of a dandelion basal rosette, and a circular sprig of broad-leafed plantain famous for its healing properties during Shakespeare's time (the bard even gave it a wry mention in *Romeo and Juliet*). Just like in my own neighborhood, the heartiest of weeds were valiantly surviving the subfreezing temperatures.

"I'm so happy," I said, as Eli and I walked back up the hill toward the path, the *Allium* tucked into my knapsack.

"I knew you'd find something," Eli said. "You're such a good spotter."

We sat down on some benches overlooking the winding footpaths and soaked in the sun, which was just breaking through the dense winter gloom. Eli poured two cups of steaming hot herbal tea from his thermos, which we slowly sipped while munching on some banana nut muffins. For the first time since my breakup, I felt almost lucky.

Foraging had a way of doing that—distracting me from the fact that I was single and in my late thirties, and, thanks to my grandmother's nagging reminders, the distinct feeling that I was running out of time.

"I have something to tell you," Eli said, looking out into the distance with watery blue eyes. He had the saddest, most compassionate, Eeyore-looking eyes of any guy I knew.

"What?" I asked, taking another bite of my muffin.

"I'm thinking of moving to Boulder—to be closer to my job."

"Oh," I said. Across the park, I could see the traffic on DeKalb Avenue through the bare trees—only a few intrepid leaves still hung onto their branches, waving in the wind. "When's this?"

"I have a business meeting next week," Eli said. "I'll be looking at apartments while I'm there."

"Oh," I repeated, feeling strangely disappointed.

"You know, I told my therapist about you," Eli continued slowly. "You and I want the same things—to have kids and to get married. . . ."

I regarded my friend. He was so cold that the tip of his nose was red. "What did she say?"

"She thinks I need time to myself, to do things for me," he said, scanning the landscape almost nervously. "But I told her—"

"She's right," I said, knowing as soon as I verbalized it that it was true.

In all of our walks together, I had toyed with the idea of getting together with Eli. He was a great foraging partner and a brilliant green architect. And despite his annoying, vegan-like eating habits, he had a spectacular laugh that needed more opportunities to escape. Plus, he was a single straight guy in New York City, and in light of that awful statistic—the one that claimed that it was easier for an unmarried woman of a certain age and education level to die in a terrorist attack than get hitched to an eligible bachelor—Eli had been looking quite appealing lately. Now that he was moving, I would never find out.

"You need to put yourself first," I said.

"Yeah, that's what my therapist said," he said, looking down at his chapped, gloveless hands.

"You need to work on your own things, before you can be there for someone else. Even me."

Eli nodded, looking a little relieved. "You're right," he said, finally smiling and downing the last of his tea. "You're pretty great."

I just smiled. Despite the sunlight on my face, I still felt cold. A few minutes later, we packed up and made our way back out of the park, heading toward the train station, where we rode the subway together a few stops before parting for our respective neighborhoods.

I was about to lose my foraging buddy, a guy who'd gone out with me even in the middle of winter to root around for strange, wild edibles when neither of us really knew what we were looking for.

I certainly didn't feel great.

Field Garlic & Hummus

Field garlic (*Allium vineale*) grows nearly year round, but it's best to pick it in early spring when the new shoots come out. Make sure you collect the freshest specimens you can find: shoots that stand straight up and are about the size of chives. Older shoots are darker, larger, and more sinewy, and bend from their own weight. That said, I've also used older field garlic bundled into a bouquet garni for vegetable stock.

(*Note:* Beware of poisonous lookalikes such as star-of-Bethlehem and fly poison, which also have small white bulbs, but lack the characteristic "garlic" fragrance.)

This makes a wonderful appetizer using either your favorite

hummus recipe or brand (I've included mine made from dried chickpeas; when time is limited, I use canned).

>> **Yields 2 pints**

> 1 cup dried garbanzo beans, soaked overnight
>   (or 3 cups reconstituted beans)
>
> 4 cups water
>
> 2 garlic cloves, peeled
>
> $1/4$ cup extra virgin olive oil
>
> $1/2$ cup tahini
>
> $1/4$ cup lemon juice, plus $1/2$ teaspoon zest
>
> $1/2$ teaspoon salt, plus more to taste
>
> $1/2$ teaspoon pepper, plus more to taste
>
> 1 teaspoon cumin seeds, bruised to release their flavor
>
> 3 to 4 sprigs of fresh field garlic strands, minced

1. Fill a large pot with the garbanzo beans and water, bring to a boil, and boil for $1^{1}/_{2}$ hours or until beans are thoroughly cooked (they should mush up easily with a fork). Drain, reserving at least $3/4$ cup of cooking liquid.

2. Mince and mash the garlic cloves into a fine paste.

3. Combine the garbanzos, garlic, most of the reserved cooking liquid, extra virgin olive oil, tahini, lemon juice and zest, and the salt and pepper into a food processor until smooth. If the hummus is too thick, add a bit more reserved liquid, until it has the desired consistency. Taste for seasoning, and add more salt and pepper if desired. Add the cumin, reserving some as garnish. Place hummus in a large serving bowl.

4. Garnish with the field garlic and place it in the center, along with reserved cumin.

4

Mushroom of Immortality

Reishi (*Ganoderma lucidum*)

The Christmas before, my ordinarily nimble grandmother—the same woman who climbed four flights of
stairs during the last blackout, who had been living on her own
ever since my grandfather passed away from colon cancer more
than a decade ago—returned home from our family gathering and collapsed in the front hall. She felt her heart racing
so loudly it flooded her ears, and she couldn't take a complete
breath. She wasn't sure how long she remained there, but at
some point, she was able to crawl across the carpet toward my
grandfather's old armchair and lean against the worn seat.

Since then, she'd been surviving on a new cocktail of drugs
designed to keep her alive.

I was taking a break from working on my field garlic article
when I called Grandma at her apartment.

"My chest—is jumping," she said, sounding like she was hiccuping. "I don't—know why."

"It's okay, Grams," I said, grabbing my jacket from a hook in the hallway. "Just hang tight, breathe deep, and I'll be there."

I arrived in Flushing in under half an hour, letting myself into her apartment with my key, shaking off my wet coat and boots in her foyer.

Grandma was sitting on the love seat, an embroidered American flag blanket across her lap. Her chest was pumping up and down. "Why—is this happening?" she said, her chest nearly hitting her chin before jerkily collapsing.

I had never seen my grandmother look scared before—angry, yes, and sad to the point of tears at my grandfather's funeral, but never afraid.

"Try to breathe slowly," I said, heading toward the kitchen. "I'll bring you some water."

The jumpy-chest phenomenon subsided within the hour to just a low set of tremors, after which I called my mother. The doctor had my grandmother on a new set of meds, which she had just started taking. "I'll call her doctor," my mother said over the phone. "Maybe we'll cut her pills in half and see how that goes."

Grandma was already on heart medication, high blood pressure medicine, and a blood thinner. I worried about this new combination of drugs as I sat down on the love seat with her. The family suspected that her fall was the beginning of a real decline, and there was now talk about putting her in an assisted-living facility or hiring an aide. One of my uncles wanted her to give away her money and go on Medicaid, but my grandmother, a dyed-in-the-wool Republican, had worked too hard saving and scrimping and hiding money away from my grandfather's ready gambling hands to go on public assistance.

"How're you feeling now?" I asked, once the tremors had dissipated.

"Okay," she said, warily. Then, waving a wizened hand in the direction of the kitchen, "There's noodles and wonton in the fridge—and lots of good things that you'll like."

That was where Grandma was so similar to Grandpa. Even in the midst of a personal crisis, she was still concerned about whether or not I had enough to eat.

"Tell me what happened, before you collapsed," I said, looking at her feet. Her legs were swollen from her ankles up to her thighs, despite her pantyhose. "Anything unusual?"

"We came home and your mother could only find parking a few blocks away," she said. "You know how impatient she gets—as we were walking she yelled at me to hurry up."

For a moment, I could barely hear my grandmother recounting how she pushed through the front door of her apartment that Christmas evening, her collapse, her difficulty breathing. I was so mad at my mother that I was having difficulty breathing myself.

"How've you been doing?" my grandmother said, suddenly cocking her head and fixing me with her good eye. "Have you been going out?"

This was code for "Are you dating?"—a difficult subject between us. The last time we had talked about my love life, my grandmother became angry at me for breaking up with Robert—despite having berated me for a year about what his intentions were, and how he was simply leading me on. ("I don't understand—you people get so close, then bam—nothing. Can't you work something out?" she had yelled.)

"I'm taking a bit of a break," I said, looking down at the worn carpet. I hadn't been on a date in months. "I need to figure some things out."

"Well, don't wait too long," she said pointedly, sitting back in her seat. Despite the fact that she was nearly blind in one eye, my grandmother always found a good enough vantage point to make an assessment. "You're not getting any younger, you know."

I just nodded, trying not to roll my eyes like a teenager.

My best friend from college often described my dating life as largely trying to fit a square peg into a round hole. When it was long obvious to everyone else that it was time to walk away, I would still be there trying out different ways to make the relationship work. Often I would find myself dialing boyfriend X's phone number, in a futile attempt to quell the anxiety that was making my palms suddenly sweaty and my breathing jagged to the point of hyperventilation. My friends would look on, after having counseled me for hours over the benefits of ending the relationship, shaking their heads in disbelief. *The round hole and the square peg.*

But these days, I was determined to do things differently, on my own terms. And if that meant a hiatus from dating until I could figure things out, then that's how it was going to be. This would have been great a few years ago, only my grandmother was right—I was now thirty-eight, with my fortieth birthday looming in the not-too-distant future.

By the time I'd returned to Brooklyn, I was pissed. Patience wasn't a family strong suit, but my mother's feelings of being overwhelmed and then taking it out on my ninety-one-year-old grandmother was unacceptable. I threw my keys down onto the hallway table.

I was going to call her up as soon as I arrived, but it was cold in the apartment and I decided to first make some tea. I'd plucked some reddish-brown reishi mushrooms from the base of a weeping willow in Central Park, and they were still sitting in the bottom of my refrigerator. After twenty minutes of heating the *Ganoderma lucidum* on the stove, a smell like old leathery shoes began to fill up the room.

I'd initially learned about reishis on a walk with Steve Brill, who had mentioned their cancer-fighting properties. My *National Audubon Society Field Guide to North American Mushrooms* by Gary Lincoff listed many names for *Ganoderma lucidum*, including *lingzhi* or *ling chih*. In China, it was referred to as the "Mushroom of Immortality" or "Herb of Spiritual Potency," and had been revered since the Chin dynasty (221–206 B.C.). Wikipedia noted its role as a fighter of cancer, tumors, and HIV, and also as a supreme immunity boost and a liver tonic. Reading through its dizzying list of beneficial properties, including being good for the heart, reishi rather seemed to me like the number-one son of Chinese medicine. I'd seen these mushrooms in Chinese pharmacies before, where they sold for upward of $20 a pound, but had otherwise overlooked them.

Scientists were finding evidence that confirmed reishi's benefits, including that reishi extract acted on the immune system, worked against the herpes virus, helped to lower cholesterol, and stopped cell proliferation. According to University of Wisconsin mycologist Tom Volk, who profiled a different fungus every month on his website, *Ganoderma lucidum* also seemed to have an anti-tumor, anti-inflammatory effect. But experiments using the mushroom had been done on lab animals only, with no long-term clinical trials on humans yet available.

I turned on my desk lamp and studied a long-stemmed specimen. The reishi was light in my hands, like a piece of driftwood, and curiously pierced by a blade of grass. (How on earth had a piece of grass wormed its way through a tough reishi mushroom?) Wondering what it looked like on the inside, I took out a giant serrated kitchen knife and a cutting board and attempted to saw my way through it.

It took fifteen hand-cramping minutes to hack off a piece the size of a tablespoon. Inside, the reishi smelled earthy and suede-like, with deep orangey-brown striations reminiscent of the mountains of Arizona's Painted Desert. I realized, after shaking my hand out, that the tender blade of grass couldn't have penetrated *Ganoderma lucidum*'s tough flesh. The reishi, in its slow-growing and methodical way, must have simply grown *around* it.

An hour later, my boil yielded a clear, brownish red tea that smelled like a cross between an old shoe and a locker room, with a squirt of lemon.

I poured myself a cup, watching the curls of steam rise in the air. Outside my kitchen window, two nesting pigeons were huddled together, each under its own separate wings. Before I moved away to attend graduate school, I spent Christmas evenings with my grandmother. I used to be the one pushing her cart and helping her into the apartment, later sorting out all the presents. But now I was independent and had a car—one that she'd helped me to purchase—and instead of helping out that night, I had driven home directly to Brooklyn, leaving my mother alone to do it.

I didn't call my mother to take her to task. Instead, I took a sip of my reishi tea.

It was hot and bitter, the bitterest liquid that I had ever tasted. I stood there and watched the snow falling onto my drafty windows, making a white seal inches thick against the bottom of the frame.

When I was a child, Grandma was my guru.

While Grandpa expanded the ever-widening reaches of my palate with culinary delights, it was Grandma who gave me lessons on life. Despite advancing arthritis, she was the one who taught me how to sew white buttons on a square of pink gingham, and later how to make a basting stitch to temporarily hem pants; how to knit a never-ending scarf using needles larger than my forearms while my mother's marriage to my stepfather slowly unraveled; how to create giant macramé wall hangings from gold yarn. She showed me how to type on her IBM Selectric typewriter, and for days I wrote, "The quick brown fox jumped over the lazy dog" in ALL CAPS because it was easier for her to see the letters.

Grandma was the first person to ride the subway with me into Manhattan and back home to Queens, providing the tokens and carefully going over how to read the map. (Real New Yorkers knew whether to stand at the back or the front of the train to get to their transfer points or exits.) I was to sit on the subway with my knees drawn tightly together and my ankles crossed, and told never to talk with my hands. "It isn't ladylike," she said.

Born in Chinatown on the crooked elbow of Mott Street, Grandma was the smarty-pants of her family. The salutatorian at her K-8 public school, she performed Chinese opera in front of audiences when she was sixteen and later attended Westerleigh, a competitive public high school on par with Stuyvesant, only Westerleigh was co-ed. She was the first woman in our family to attend college—Hunter, when it was an all-girls' school in the Bronx.

On the weekends when I stayed over, reading books in bed and overindulging in television, I marveled that she had been a math major in college, whereas I struggled with fractions and later, elementary algebra.

While the kitchen was clearly Grandpa's domain, on Sunday mornings Grandma and I took over, baking batches of blueberry muffins and angel food cake that made the whole house smell like a confectionary. By the time my mother came to pick me up at the end of the weekend, there was rarely a muffin or any cake left. "You should have gotten here sooner," I always said.

One of my favorite childhood games was playing the part of her beautician. Our Saturday night ritual involved Jergens lotion, a fine-toothed metal comb, and a shoe box full of pink curlers. In addition to asking her myriad questions about my father, I separated her salt-and-pepper hair into inch-long sections, wrapping each hair cluster around my finger with the comb, and learned about life.

"How did you get so gray?" I asked, before rolling her hair into a curler and snapping it shut.

"It's what happens when you get old," she answered, watching her television program—a cop show that featured a car chase at the end of every episode.

"What was Grandpa like when you first met him?"

"Nice and quiet," she said, barely blinking from behind her glasses. "Now he won't shut up."

"What does it feel like to have a baby?" The list of questions was exhaustive and never-ending, but if Grandma felt annoyed she never let it show.

At this, she paused. "It hurts, but then when you see that cute little face, you forget all about the pain," she said, smiling.

I didn't believe her. I couldn't imagine passing a small creature the size of a baby watermelon from the area where I peed, and forgetting about the pain just because I was looking down at a bawling infant.

At bedtime, we snuggled up together in her queen-size bed.

Grandma was a warm and fleshy bundle in matching two-piece pajamas, with a tissue tucked inside a rubber band on her wrist.

On cold winter nights, the air would filter through the back windows of the house, sounding like the Indian war calls in John Wayne movies.

"Grandma?" I asked, holding her hand under the covers. Her wedding band—with its row of tiny diamonds—was cool and slightly uneven under my fingers. "Do you love me?"

"Yes, I love you."

"Why? Why do you love me?"

"Because you're my granddaughter. And just because."

"Because what?"

"I love you just because I do."

"Are you sure?" I asked. "Are you sure you love me? If I weren't your granddaughter, would you still love me?"

"Yes, I'd love you. Now go to sleep."

This conversation played liked a rerun every weekend. I never tired of asking, and to my grandmother's credit, she always answered in the affirmative. Often, with my feet resting against her legs, it was the only way that I could fall asleep.

As close as we'd been when I was a girl, my grandmother and I also experienced our fair share of arguments. The most difficult crisis I faced with her was when I was getting to know Stanley, years before I started foraging. My grandfather had just lost ten pounds from the cancer that was expanding in his intestines, and I was trying to confront my old personal issues by forging a relationship with my dad.

That year marked the first time I spent Father's Day with him instead of with my grandfather. I didn't tell Grandma—

making up some excuse about being away that weekend—but by accident I left my monthly planner at their apartment. When my grandmother discovered it, she was livid.

"All we did for you! This is how you repay us?" she shouted over the phone when I called. "Who took care of you when you were little? Who changed your diapers?"

"Grandma, I didn't mean—"

"I don't want to hear it!" she yelled. "You don't come here—you don't call here anymore!"

When my grandfather came on the line, Grandma's shouting was still audible in the background.

"She's been acting crazy all day," he said.

"Please talk to her. I'm so sorry—I didn't mean—"

"I don't understand her," he said, turning away from the phone to tell her to calm down in Chinese. Then, "You'd better not call," he said, hanging up.

I immediately called again, but the phone kept ringing and ringing.

My grandmother refused to talk to me for three months, and in that time I was persona non grata. I was banned from the household, and every time I called, I was met with a click and the sound of the dial tone. Worse than her formidable anger was her refusal to let me see my dying grandfather.

Finally, my mother and I staged an intervention. One morning, we walked into the apartment together like a united force. I was grateful to have my mom there by my side. Even though Grandma barely said hello at the door, she didn't stop me from entering—she just stepped aside and begrudgingly let me in.

My grandfather was sitting in his easy chair, skinnier than when I'd last seen him, his hair thinner from radiation treatments.

"Why did you do it?" Grandpa asked, his normally resonant

voice barely audible, even from where I was sitting, on the low living-room steps by his feet.

"I needed to, Grandpa," I said. "I've always wanted to know who he was."

Growing up, I was pretty certain that when I met my father, Grandpa—the Stanley-hater who became red-faced whenever his name was mentioned—would be the angry one, and my grandma the voice of reason. I didn't expect it to be the other way around.

"It was because of you," I said slowly. "You've always been a father to me, and now we're losing you." I started to cry, but I forced myself to keep on talking. "I want to be a parent one day—like you and Grandma. But how can I be a good parent if I don't even know or understand what went on between my own?"

I sat there crying. Crying was traditionally a source of embarrassment in our family. Like many Chinese people bewildered by sudden strong emotions, my grandparents would often react to my tears by saying things like, "Why are you so upset?" and "Stop that!," regarding me as if I were a waitress who'd just spilled water onto their laps. I always felt truly American at times like that—I could easily cry a river when I was upset—and their attempts at getting me to stop always only furthered the cause.

But this time, my grandfather just looked solemn and nodded. He didn't try to stop it.

Less than a year after Grandpa died, I was admitted to the master's program in creative writing at Johns Hopkins in Baltimore, and for the very first time, I lived several states away from my family.

I felt my grandfather's presence even down there, though, especially after I first moved and was walking across an empty campus. I could feel him watching me from the wide, open sky, although I didn't quite believe in heaven.

My family members, especially my grandmother, were extremely supportive. Before I left, they pooled money together to help with my living expenses so that I didn't have to work while studying. Only Stanley didn't come through with all that he had promised.

I was lonely those first few weeks in Baltimore, but I talked to my grandmother every weekend. Although we were more than two hundred miles away from each other, she and I often had dreams about Grandpa on the same nights.

One morning, Grandma asked me about my father. "Do you ever speak to him?"

Even if I had, I knew better than to say yes. The last time I'd seen him was when he tried to run away from me on the street.

"No, Grandma," I said into the phone that morning, pulling back the curtains from the bay windows. My new Baltimore apartment was far from being finished, but when the light hit the hardwood floors and my Victorian furniture, it looked almost pretty. "I haven't spoken to Stanley in a while."

"Good," she said. "Because he isn't a nice person. You know, when your mother was pregnant, he wanted her to get an abortion."

There's a drawback to antique furniture—when you suddenly needed to take a seat, the hardness could be shocking. I sat there, my butt growing numb against the edge of the chair.

"He would have made her go through with it, too, if she hadn't stood up for herself. If we hadn't supported her decision," my grandmother continued, as if she were complaining to a friend, as if we weren't talking about my parents aborting me.

Even though my parents were engaged when my mother became pregnant, Stanley didn't want more children. I'd known this for years and suspected he'd pressured her about getting an abortion—at that time an illegal, dangerous back-alley operation—but hearing my grandmother's words stung. No one in my family had ever verbalized it before.

"I had to meet with him and his lawyer to convince him to marry her," she said. "He swore up and down that he would never set eyes on the child as long as he lived."

The child.

"Grandma, I gotta go," I said, the words fluttering in my throat like paper going up a chimney.

I waited for her cursory "Okay, talk to you later," before hanging up.

For several moments, I sat in my hard chair by the window, feeling nothing but a slight numbing chill as dust particles swirled in the light before settling onto the floor.

When I entered the bathroom, getting undressed for my shower, tears were running down my face. Sitting on the edge of my claw-foot bathtub with the ancient plumbing, I turned the levers so that both hot and cold water ran full blast. The water hit the curtain.

I knew what my grandmother was trying to do. Mix the cement and hit the nail securely on the coffin. Make sure I never spoke again to that man who'd betrayed the family. That traitor, that rascal who'd ruined her daughter.

But Stanley was still my father. It didn't seem fair that I had to bear the brunt of what he did so many years ago. Nor was it my fault that I wanted to know him—who he was and where I had come from, what I was or wasn't missing out on all those years.

When the temperature was right, I stepped into the shower.

Hearing my grandmother's words echoing in my ears, I felt a pain as sharp as a physical blade in my chest. My tears dissolved in the water and ran down the length of my body. I was a mess, a red-hot mess.

That's when I really started crying—big, sobbing torrents that if any family members were to witness would probably make them turn away in Chinese embarrassment. I could practically taste the metallic edge separating life and death like a razor in my mouth.

I turned, letting the water hit me squarely on the back of the neck and shoulders. For better or worse, my birth was forever entangled with the moment of Stanley's disappearance. And even if it wasn't true that my parents had separated because of me, it was a fact that he'd disappeared and didn't want to have anything to do with me then, or even now.

Standing under the beating showerhead, I could have been angry at my grandmother for speaking the unspoken. There's a fine line between being informative and sheer manipulation, and that morning, she'd jumped into enemy territory.

But all I knew was that I loved her. And when you love someone as much as I did Grandma, it was easy to empathize with her pain.

I had forgiven her by the time I'd turned off the shower—twists that made the plumbing shudder before cutting the water completely.

As I thought back on that difficult time in my life, I took a long walk through Prospect Park, warmed by my layered clothing and all the cups of reishi tea that I'd consumed. I was alone—there were no dog-walkers, nor any joggers with their frozen breath-clouds trailing behind them along the track.

There was just me, the crazy forager girl walking by herself, wrapped up in a down coat and two layers of turtlenecks.

From my vantage point on the secluded hill, I could see the road below through the spindly bared branches of oaks and maples. There were still pockets of snow nestled among the tree stumps and living roots, and I could hear the crunch of ice breaking under my feet. I followed the path down a steep incline covered with frozen foliage, sliding a little despite my boots until I was on level land again. At a small clearing, I found a fat log the length of a picnic table and made myself a seat.

Henry David Thoreau once described nature in winter as being "a cabinet of curiosities," where what remained under a "clean napkin of snow," stripped back and naked to the elements, was holy—revealing the divine presence of God. I was surrounded by tree branches, the wizened remnants of weeds and bushes, and an entire embankment still covered in snow. Under the cold gray sky, it was surprising that anything could survive such brutality.

I was looking down at my gloved hands when I noticed something underneath me. Only a few inches from where my fingers were gripping the wet bark were the soft, scalloped edges of reishi—three little *ling chih*, like dark shelves practically camouflaged in the old wood. I had no idea how long they'd been growing there, but I was shaking when I pried them loose, more from excitement than from the cold. The mushrooms ripped away easily in my hands.

I sat there on that log, marveling at the resiliency of nature and the earth's ability to provide. Even among the coldest layer of frost there were plants and mushrooms that embraced winter, as well as other, more hidden, things—roots, fungi, and seeds—all lying dormant, awaiting the arrival of spring.

Reishi Tea

Different teas require different heating methods—some leaf teas work well as infusions (steeping in boiling water with a lid over it), while others require some more heavy-duty boiling methods. Reishi mushrooms fall into the latter category.

Reishis are incredibly woody and hard mushrooms, especially when mature. I've found them growing at the base of a variety of trees throughout the city, including willows, sycamores, and pines. (They are also widely available in Chinese pharmacies.) Reishis have a beautiful reddish-brown top that often appears shellacked; flip the mushroom over and you'll find a white, porous underside that you could dent with a fingernail (*Ganoderma lucidum* is a polypore). Don't handle this side too roughly, however, as it is considered the most medicinal part of the mushroom.

I like to fill up a 3½-quart pot with enough water so that the pot is filled three-quarters of the way. Place one large reishi (or two smallish ones) white-side down; the mushrooms will float on the top. Use a medium-high flame and cover until the pot comes to a roiling boil (about 20 minutes); lower heat and cook for at least an hour, checking periodically to see that the pot has enough liquid in it.

Your tea is done when the liquid turns a clear, dark reddish-brown color, rather like ten-minute steeped oolong. Be forewarned, however, that this hefty medicinal tea is the kind of bitter that makes even Chinese grandmothers raise eyebrows.

Spring

5

A Communion with the Earth

Wood sorrel (*Oxalis montana*)

My editor, Andy, loved my field garlic story, and a few weeks later, the "Urban Forager" was born. The *Times* included two photographs: a close-up of my hands, emerging from the puffy sleeves of my coat, cradling the weedy *Allium*, and another of the plant growing near a steamy manhole cover.

On days that I wasn't teaching, I took long walks in the park. In winter, it was easy to spy the wizened forms of plants otherwise obscured by the lushness of other seasons. The forked remains of native pokeweed. The low-lying bramble of an old blackberry bush. I discovered patches of the skeletal remains of last year's knee-high garlic mustard—grabbing the chaff in my gloved hands, and blowing it out until only the spicy seeds remained.

And then, one day, as if by magic, the small shoots of tiny

crocus appeared across the city, little green buds poking out of the earth, reaching toward the sun.

No one I spoke to believed that spring had arrived. The city was still cold and wet, the air nipping New Yorkers' cheeks. While it rarely snowed anymore, the rain came down in sleety sheets against my windows, my rubber boots, even under my umbrella as I ran out of the vestibule of my brownstone, heading toward the train station, on my way to the latest lecture on technology, or singles gathering, or meeting of self-proclaimed nerdy types I'd met online.

I was back on the dating market. I went out with information technology guys who worked for major financial institutions, divorced dads who worked for the Federal Reserve or small New Jersey banks, even a political science professor whom I met while speed-dating, the latest dating phenomenon, where one had the opportunity to meet about fifteen other singles for under five minutes each.

I wore my best-foot-forward clothing—hyper-feminine clothes where every outfit was silky and red, the color of luck and Chinese brides.

My foraging habits were sometimes a conversation-halter— like a needle flying off a record. Sometimes, the stunned silence was followed by an unconvincing "How *interesting*." Only the professor, who was British and whose mother drank nettles tea, didn't seem to think that what I did was all that strange.

At the end of these dates, if the date was a particularly good one, I let the guy kiss me at the train station, at the curb after my cab pulled up, or sometimes even at my front door. But I always ran up the stairs of my apartment building alone, preferring to spend the rest of the evening reading foraging books—Euell Gibbons's *Stalking the Wild Asparagus*, the Peterson Guides to *Edible Wild Plants* and *Medicinal Plants and Herbs*, Elias and

Dykeman's *Edible Wild Plants*—hungrily devouring each page, contemplating the next plant or wild mushroom that I might be able to find.

Robert and I had met nearly two years before, on an Ivy League dating website. He was in his late forties and had a rich, deep voice—the only hint of his Southern background audible in his substitute of "Ah" for "I." He was eleven years older than I was, but I didn't really mind the age difference. Back then, I had a thing for older men.

Even though both of us were children of divorced parents, we discussed wanting marriage and kids from the start. On one of our early dates, Robert grabbed my hand across the table of a noisy restaurant and rather drunkenly declared, "I always knew that I'd have a great partner!" As I got to know him, seeing how generous and considerate he was, I was surprised that he had never been married before, that none of his previous long-term relationships had ever worked out. "Maybe they weren't the right ones for him," my girlfriends said. Only my grandmother was suspicious ("He's old enough to know what he wants by now," she insisted. "He should give you some real indication of his intentions.")

Just before New Year's Eve, three months into our relationship, Robert and I celebrated by going swing dancing with friends on the second floor of an old Irish bar, decorated for the holidays with white and silver balloons that bobbed above the heads of dancing couples. I felt glorious in a new silk-crepe dress with a stiff white crinoline. When the next song struck up, an enthusiastic swing number, Robert, dressed in a suit and suede-bottomed leather shoes, led me out to the dance floor so confidently that my skirt swung out as we paused to take our places. A woman next to us gasped in admiration. Facing Robert, nearly eye level in my good heels, I felt like the prettiest thing in the room.

Even though I had danced swing only intermittently before meeting him, I'd practiced salsa regularly in my twenties. Luckily, the art of being a good follower translated into lindy hop, swing, and even the more bluesy West Coast swing, which I enjoyed even though I sometimes fumbled over the fundamentals of shuffling backward and forward along "the slot." Robert's arms were boxy and solid, and it was fun to be held within his frame, dancing to the infectious horns of shimmering, old-timey music. Everything seemed so innocent, so much like the couples-dating my grandmother did in 1930s Chinatown. Even when I stepped out of time, I just laughed as Robert caught me back into his arms. With his experience, and my natural abilities and enthusiasm, I envisioned us jump-jive-and-wailing together, hand-in-hand, throughout our golden years.

When the song came to an end, Robert led me back to the bar, where several of his friends had congregated. There was Lena, his former dance partner, and her husband, and Robert's brother and sister-in-law and their friends.

"Want to dance?" Robert asked Lena, taking her hand. "You mind?" he asked me.

"Not at all," I said, trying to sound charitable.

Lena turned to her husband. "Dance with Ava," she said, before disappearing into the balloons and swirling skirts.

Lena's husband watched her being led away by my boyfriend with an expression like that of a forlorn pup. We danced together for one song, and when it was over, he looked relieved.

At the start of the next song, a particularly bluesy number I recalled from childhood, I began to search for signs of Robert in the crowd. A glimpse of his brown hair. The white sleeve of his dress shirt peeking out from his fine-cut suit. All I saw were random strangers.

When Robert and Lena finally returned, panting and flushed, Robert having loosened his tie, I was standing by the bar with the others, feeling a little left out. Before I could catch his eye, Robert invited his sister-in-law to dance. I stood there, watching their backs being swallowed up by the other dancers. I couldn't even pretend that I was having a good time.

I watched from the edge of the crowd, searching for some way to reorganize things back to the way the evening started—just the two of us, a couple that others might envy.

When Robert returned, sweaty and red-faced from dancing so many songs in a row, I could barely look at him. "Having fun?" I said.

"I'm going to ask Sandra to dance," he said. Sandra, his sister-in-law's best friend, was standing by the bar talking with her husband.

I suddenly flashed on a mental image of Sandra, another woman who wasn't me caught in Robert's arms. "Why?" I asked. "She looks pretty occupied to me."

"It's polite," he said.

"Why do you have to ask everyone else to dance?" I said, loud enough to be heard over the music. "No other guy in our group asks someone who's not his partner to dance."

"It's just courtesy to dance with other people—it's a way of practicing and improving your dancing."

"But what about me? I'm your date," I said. "And we've only danced together once."

"I'll dance with you after I dance with Sandra."

Even though I'd been waiting for him to ask me all night, I said, "No."

"No?"

"You don't get it," I said, and then there were tears in my eyes, because somehow that seemed the worse thing of all.

"I don't understand why you're getting so upset," he said, staring down at me through his glasses with an expression I had never seen from him before. As if someone had carved him out of granite.

"You care about what other people think more than you care about me and my feelings." As soon as I said it, I knew that I was reaching, but I desperately wanted Robert to deny it just to make me feel better.

But then there it was, another thought right behind it, like an intruder lurking in the shadows. What if it were true? What if he really cared more about others than he cared about me? Suddenly, I was back in an apartment, alone again.

"What?" he said.

"I didn't sign up for this," I said, my mouth talking faster than my brain. I knew I was being ridiculous, but I couldn't stop. "I just—I have to get out of here." Everything was going out of control and I didn't know whether to cry or bolt or do both. "I want to go home—alone."

"Where is this coming from?" he asked, suddenly sounding angry.

"I want—" I started. But in truth I didn't know what I wanted. Robert's attention? His love, though we weren't at the point where we were using that word? "I'm sorry, I just have to get out of here," I said. Over the door was a red exit sign; a flood of people were trying to get in. "Can we please go home?"

"Okay," he said. His face looked set—not angry or curious, just set, like pudding after an hour in the refrigerator.

As he fumbled around for our coats, tightly jammed between a hundred others on a long metal coat rack, a flood of remorse kicked in. I put my hand on Robert's arm before it was too late.

"Let's stay," I said, quickly.

He looked at me oddly, as if he were staring at a stranger.

"Look, I know I got upset, but I feel better now," I said as slowly as I could. I wanted to appear calm, reasonable. "I felt like you checked out and I couldn't tell where you were."

"I'm right *here*," he said, not bothering to cover up his annoyance.

"I'm sorry," I said. "I was just upset, but I'm not anymore." I tried to put on a convincing smile. "Put the coat down—let's stay."

I tugged on Robert's sleeve and we joined the rest of the group, who were still chatting away at the bar. No one had noticed our exchange, or if they did, they didn't let on.

Later, when other women asked him to dance, Robert declined. We looked like we were having fun on the surface— dancing a few songs together, including a West Coast one where Robert's hand lingered about my waist in moments. But even though I loved the music, and spun around as smoothly as I could, even the edges of my new dress seemed a little flatter.

The next morning, when Robert woke up, he could barely look at me. I was already awake, sitting up against the pillows, the room filled with a cold, austere light—an overcast day. Across the river, New Jersey was a gray smudge. A barge floated across the icy water.

I touched Robert's shoulder. "I want to apologize."

"What was that last night?" he said, propping up on one arm. "Never in a million years would I have expected that of you."

"I'm sorry," I said.

"Is this a normal occurrence?"

I just sighed. "Look, I panicked. I don't want to make excuses, but there are a few things you should know about me. It's pretty old, and hurts to even talk about."

I took a deep breath. Robert knew that I'd been raised by a single mom, but he didn't know about the parade of boyfriends or the weekends I spent with my grandparents, comforting myself with food.

I didn't know where to start, so I mentioned a time when I woke up in the apartment alone in the wee hours of the morning.

My mother had gone out dancing, which wasn't unusual—she'd been doing that ever since she and my stepdad had separated. I had been asleep for hours, when something woke me—whether it was a car alarm or a shouting neighbor, or even the sound of a truck rumbling down the nearby turnpike, I wasn't certain. I crawled out of bed in my pajamas and walked into the hallway.

A single light was on in the living room, casting shadows onto the floor, and the radio was on low, set to a top-40 station. Since it was after midnight, they were playing cool jazz and R&B.

I backtracked to my mother's bedroom. Her bed was covered with several slinky outfits she'd decided against wearing.

Back in the hallway, I stared up at the apartment door and the deadbolt lock.

I'd never heard of anyone breaking into our building, but suddenly I was compelled to make the apartment as secure as possible. I dragged as much furniture as I could under my arms across the wood floors, including a wooden chair that I could barely lift, and a silver stepladder. I had some notion that the ladder, with its rubber-gripped feet, unfolded and propped up against the door, would be an adequate barrier against intruders.

It was only then, with the door barricaded, that I could safely go back to bed and fall asleep again.

"How old were you?" Robert asked.

"Nine," I said, looking down, not wanting to see his face wrinkling in concern.

"My mom used to party a lot," I said. "When I got older, she sometimes told me, 'If we run into anyone I know, just say you're my *sister*.'"

"Have you talked to her about this?" he asked.

"She doesn't remember a lot of it." I looked down at the floor, covered with clothes and pillows. "She admits she was crazy back then, but that's it."

"What did your grandparents think?"

"They didn't know. I didn't think to tell them—I just thought that was what all single mothers did," I said, finally looking up. Even though we were on opposite sides of the bed, I could see my partial reflection in his pale blue eyes.

"When you were dancing with other women, it made me feel alone. I freaked out," I said, fingering the covers. "I know for you it's a social thing, but for me it really triggers something deep."

"I can see how this would still affect you," Robert said, reaching for his jeans. "Maybe you should talk to your mother again."

I shrugged. When someone has forgotten what she's done—filed it under the era of her "Crazy Years"—what's the point?

Robert leaned over and kissed me on the forehead. It felt like hot air being released from a pressurized tank.

But even as we got dressed and headed down to the local diner for breakfast, a nagging, residual feeling of dread and fear persisted throughout the rest of the day. It lasted even as I got dressed for our New Year's Eve celebration, sliding on my heels and pinning back my hair, wearing a brand-new beaded, floor-length, cream-colored dress that prompted observations from other revelers at the swanky Union Square restaurant we were dining at that I looked like "a bride." Even as we sat at our table, after a meal of sea scallops and chocolate mousse, sipping champagne, yelling the countdown, watching the sparkly confetti fly down like fluttery snowflakes from the ceiling, and suddenly everyone kissing and drunkenly stomping on balloons, I couldn't quite shake it. For I knew the real secret of which every kid with missing parents was aware. If you confronted the parent that stayed, they might decide to permanently leave, too. And even though I'm a gambler's granddaughter, I was never willing to risk that.

Robert and I appeared to grow closer after that—vacationing together in the Dominican Republic and taking trips down to New Orleans to see his family. But as the seasons progressed, our relationship began to stall. He attended national dance competitions on his own, preferring to dance with other women rather than take me. When I raised the possibilities of our moving in together that summer, instead of being excited over the prospects, Robert simply shut down.

On our anniversary, when no ring or talk about moving our relationship further appeared, I made a decision to honor myself and my own desires. Instead of fighting with Robert or causing a big scene over why he didn't love me as much as he should have—as I'd done in most of my other major relationships—I packed up all my things from his apartment and left.

⟡

"I'm back dating again, Grandma," I said, letting myself into her apartment and dumping my overnight bag into the foyer. Grandma's new daytime aide was preparing to leave; she waved, closing the door. "But I'm not going to settle down until I find someone who's really good—someone who's offering a real commitment," I declared, *i.e., I'm not making the same mistake that I did with Robert.*

My grandmother was sitting in her customary place—on the love seat in front of the television at the far end of the living room. She had recently begun losing many of her motor functions, and her head nodded forward, as if she had fallen asleep in a rocking chair.

I rushed over, alarmed, but just as I reached her, my grandmother righted herself. Even though she claimed that she wasn't in any pain, it hurt to see her like this.

"I'm glad to hear it," she said without looking up, her voice thick with something other than sleep. Then a long pause, as if she'd conked out, before picking her head up like a train passenger approaching a station.

"Because that . . ." she said (rocking forward, then back again), " . . . has been . . ." (forward, then back), " . . . your downfall."

Later that night, after dinner, I helped my grandmother, now using a metal-framed walker, down into the sunken living room, where we sat on her love seat together. Her hearing aids weren't working that well, so I turned up the volume on her favorite evening game show, the one where they spin the giant wheel.

While she nodded out, I hunkered down over a book that I was teaching the following day.

Suddenly, I felt a poke at my shoulder.

"I've been meaning to tell you something," my grandmother said, her eyes transformed back to their former alertness, her head surprisingly upright.

"What?"

"This," she said.

Mimicking how I was reading with my head down, she shook her head and frowned, waving her finger. *No, no.*

Then she lifted her fingers under her chin, indicating that it be raised high, until she looked as regal as the queen.

Confused, I mirrored her from over my book. "That's right," she said smiling, before her head slowly sank down again.

Although she was dying, my grandmother still thought it was important to improve my posture—she didn't want it to look like her granddaughter had a double chin.

Over the sound of her heavy breathing, the applause from the television audience was sudden and intense.

That night, I tried to fall asleep on the couch, listening to my grandmother's intermittent moaning from her bedroom. It sounded like slow torture. While she had earlier assured me that she wasn't in any pain—that it was simply a way to soothe herself, the way an infant cries before falling asleep—it was still upsetting.

When I was a child, long before I understood death first-hand, I used to wonder how I'd feel when my grandparents passed away. I had such a small family trinity that just thinking about their dying made me fear that I was going to shatter like the myriad pieces of a dropped rice bowl, or the broken car-window glass that littered the streets of the Bushwick, Brooklyn, school district where my mother taught.

I started to cry, thinking about losing her. With both grandparents gone, there would only be my mother and me left.

This made me cry even harder. I was so consumed by my own grief, sobbing in the semidarkness of the living room, the only other sound that of the occasional car driving down the block, that it took a few minutes before I realized my grandmother's moaning had stopped.

I held my breath, listening for her, ready to jump up from the couch.

After a few heart-stopping moments, Grandma's moans became audible again, this time like an infant's whimpers.

"It hasn't happened yet," I said, suddenly able to breathe again. "I still have her, she's still here with us."

But there was no one in the living room except me and the streetlight projected on the walls.

My friend Heidi, a former Chinatown labor activist and fellow native New Yorker, lived in a giant communal brownstone in Fort Greene, Brooklyn, a half block away from where Eli and I had discovered the field garlic. I'd been coming to Heidi's home throughout the years for parties ever since we graduated from college—we were both CUNY alumnae—but this was the first time I was over to snoop around her backyard for wild edibles.

I had just stepped out into the morning light, blinking hard and staring across the great expanse of the backyard—one of three linked gardens shared by several residents. My editor, Andy, had suggested that I file an edible plant profile every other week, but while city weeds were prolific, I wasn't certain that I had the skills to find them so early in the season. Even Heidi's well-tended vegetable and flowering patches were mostly filled with twigs and brown earth.

I was wondering how I was going to find anything growing to write about, when I noticed something small and innocuous in the claw-foot bathtub filled with soil that Heidi used as a container bed for growing basil. It was a three-leaved shamrock nestled near the tub's edge.

I peered down at the tiny weed before calling her over. "Do you know this plant?" I asked.

"Clover?" Heidi said, wiping her gloved hands onto her jeans.

"Wood sorrel," I said, remembering the first time I'd tasted its burst of flavor on a foraging tour, and how it transformed Willy Wonka–like in my mouth.

Wood sorrel (*Oxalis montana*), aka shamrocks, common wood sorrel, hearts, sourgrass, or sours, can be found across the eastern part of the United States as far west as Minnesota and south to Georgia. It has folded, heart-shaped leaves, which flutter open and closed depending on the time of day, rather like slow-moving butterflies. From May to July, it produces pretty yellow flowers in the New York area.

A member of the Oxalidaceae family, wood sorrel is reputedly what St. Patrick held up as an emblem of the trinity. Native American tribes have used various related Oxalises to treat thirst, nausea, and cramps.

Not to be confused with the plant used in the sweet, red Caribbean drink ("sorrel"), delicate wood sorrel has a zippy tanginess that is pleasantly citrusy. Another wild edible, sheep's sorrel (*Rumex acetosella*), has a similar flavor, but the plants are related in common name only.

Heidi ate a small leaf and considered it. "Hmm," she said, smiling suddenly. "Very lemony."

The last time I'd tasted wood sorrel was on a blustery day the previous November, when my family gathered to honor the tenth anniversary of my grandfather's death at his gravesite on Long Island.

I had only recently broken up with Robert, and my grandmother still refused to talk to me since we'd had a big argument about it over the phone.

"I don't understand. Doesn't he still have feelings for you? How can he just walk away like that?" my grandmother had said from her Flushing apartment. Even though she was born in Manhattan, her Queens-inflected accent came out in an emphasis of certain phrases of loss like "walk away." "Don't you still have feelings for him?" she continued. "You spent a whole year together!"

"It's for the best, Grandma," I said, pacing my living room while on my cell, trying to comfort her like some kid of divorce, only that was my role. "Robert would've dragged this on forever."

"I don't understand you people—you get so close and then, bam—it's over?" she said.

I just rolled my eyes and paced the living room, which wasn't far—mostly I walked from my writing desk to the love seat and back again.

"What's he looking for, anyway—you're a nice girl, with a good education. What, he thinks he can do better?" she said, needling into all my soft spots. In my grandmother's 1930s view of dating, being a good girl with a degree was all the armor a woman needed against the inanities of modern dating. Only it wasn't any insurance for my mother when she met my father, or for myself.

"What—he's just going to move on to the next person, forget you, and that's it?"

"I don't know, Grams," I said. I could feel myself getting upset. "I can't hold a gun to his head. Besides, you were the one who kept telling me that he should know by now."

"I don't understand—you people get so close and then, bam—nothing," she said. Whenever she couldn't comprehend something upsetting, my grandmother repeated herself like a tape loop. "Can't you work something out?"

"No, we can't, Grandma," I said. "You know, your questions are really starting to upset me."

"*I'm* upsetting you?" she said, punctuating her subject-nouns with all the sass and attitude of a woman raised in lower Manhattan. "I'm sorry I asked—I'm just trying to help."

"Oh, come on," I said, staring at the whitewashed brick wall in my living room. "Don't be like that."

"I'm on your side, not his."

"Well, he wasn't going to do anything," I said. "He was just wasting my time."

"You can't just blame him—you stayed in it, too, you know," she said matter-of-factly.

"Great," I said, feeling my cheeks flush. "Now it's all my fault—me and my expiring eggs should've left earlier."

"Now you're just feeling sorry for yourself. You stayed, too, even though you knew better."

"Great," I repeated, my voice quivering as it always did whenever I was about to get really upset. "You know, I've never seen a good relationship in this family, and now it's all *my* fault."

As soon as I said it, I realized that I'd gone too far. I was referring to my parents' failed relationships, but Grams thought I was including her and Grandpa, too.

"Forget about it!" my grandmother said, her old-timey Manhattan accent suddenly shifting, inexplicably, to elongated, television Brooklynese as she started yelling. "That's your problem. No one can tell you anything—you don't listen to anybody. So fuggedaboutit! Forget I even mentioned it. Fuggedaboutit! Fuggedaboutit!"

Before I could protest, I heard the click of the phone as she hung up.

Over the course of the next few weeks, in the middle of the worst financial crisis in America since the Great Depression, Lehman Brothers collapsed, and my grandmother lost six figures in the process. Even though we hadn't spoken since our argument, I sent a check to help with her expenses. Perhaps it was a kind of unspoken apology of sorts: *Sorry I hurt your feelings; sorry I implied your relationship with Grandpa was no good; sorry I'm a failure as a granddaughter and can't seem to maintain a meaningful, lasting relationship with a man.*

All of this had gone unsaid, but I knew that she would get it. We never apologized in our family. We just held it in, and got mad at each other until the point where one of us exploded. Eventually, we accepted the other person back in, but not before making him or her suffer with long silences, skeptical looks, and monosyllabic answers. Grudges were held for months, or in special cases, decades.

Although I'd never heard from her, the check had cleared.

It was a cold and windy autumn day when my family gathered at the top of the cemetery hill in Great Neck, Long Island, to pay our respects to my grandfather. My grandmother, who was ignoring me, refused my outstretched hand—instead, she shakily made her way down the hill holding on to my aunt and aided by her wooden cane. I made my way slowly behind them, past the Japanese maples and stone benches, weaving around the headstones. Ten years before, the expanse of the grounds was grassy and open. As the years went by, the churchyard had become densely crowded, filled with the "new" Asians—the Parks and Kims and Lees—and now there were headstones to either side of ours. Even though we were in the middle of suburbia, the cemetery resembled my grandparents' apartment building.

We arrived in front of my grandfather's grave, gathered in a semicircle. I watched my mother and cousin clear away the old stuffed bears and angels decorating his headstone. We didn't leave roasted meats and fruit like other Chinese families— just stuffed animals and the occasional potted plant. I didn't know if Grandpa, who liked to place porcelain bodhisattvas in strategic places around the living room because he believed in good feng shui, would have been appalled at the next genera- tions' American-ness, although I suspected that he was already used to us.

Since his death, the family had grown larger and larger, and farther and farther apart—half of my married cousins had moved farther out on Long Island, and mostly traveled to their in-laws for the holidays. Only my uncle cooked delicious, all- encompassing meals, and he did it only for certain times of the year; moreover, it was mostly Italian or American, and rarely Chinese.

I was staring down at my grandfather's plot, tuning out my family, trying to swallow the hard lump that had formed in my throat, when I noticed something: here and there among the blades of grass were pockets of edible weeds, tenacious sur- vivors of the groundskeeper's lawnmower. While the others continued talking around me, everything seemed to go out of focus except the ground, which suddenly appeared strangely alive, and for the first time I noticed clusters of delicate wood sorrel and their cleft, heart-shaped leaves gently opening under the November skies.

Without thinking, I dropped to my knees. The wood sorrel really did resemble small shamrocks, and taking a bite was a bright and lemony relief. I ate one sprig, followed by another, and then another, hungry for the citrusy burst on my tongue. Then, I started to cry. I cried over my grandmother's wall of silence, my failed relationship with Robert, and for all of the former kids without fathers who no longer had their grandfather substitutes. I cried until my tears made the vegetation under my clogs wet like rain and it seemed as though everything had gone quiet. When I finished, all that I could see were the patches of wood sorrel, larger than my outspread hands and all along Grandpa's grave, one small bite at a time. It was sharp, pleasant, and surprising.

I closed my eyes, thankful for what was there beneath our feet. I thanked the earth for producing tiny tart plants, thriving weeds, and woody medicinal mushrooms that steadfastly grew around pokey blades of grass. When my grandfather was alive he had taught me how to eat—*dong gu*, winter melon, *po nay, dong quai*. *This* was good for digestion, *that* was good for after giving birth. It was information to last an entire lifetime. And here he was, a decade later, gently instructing and still providing, silently transforming the earth into a living, breathing salad.

Wood Sorrel Micro-Greens

Wood sorrel is best eaten fresh and on the day on which it is collected. A bright and lemony surprise on the palate, use it as you would any kind of supermarket micro-green. I enjoy wood sorrel as a topping for poached salmon or spring and summer salads. Because it is one of the few wild edibles that can grow throughout the winter—I've seen wood sorrel peeking out from under snow banks in the middle of Manhattan's Upper East Side—it is a nutritious treat when market vegetables pale that time of year.

Soak wood sorrel in a bowl of water to clean. If wilting, spriggy *Oxalis montana* will perk up in a matter of minutes. Please don't try to cook it, as wood sorrel disintegrates at the faintest touch of heat.

Note: Because wood sorrel is high in oxalic acid, which can interfere with calcium metabolism, it should be avoided by those with kidney issues, rheumatism, or gout.

6

Gifts of Spring

Garlic mustard (*Alliaria petiolata*)

As the days grew warmer and lengthened and the daffodils sprouted across the five boroughs, my grandmother's mood improved even while her health remained shaky. I took several trips out to Queens, baking blueberry muffins in her oven, the way we used to nearly every weekend when I was a kid. Only this time I was in the adult role—lighting and preheating the oven, placing the tray of wet mix on the hot rack, then pulling it out some twenty-five minutes later. Together, we sat in the increasingly smaller moments of her lucidity, eating the steaming-hot muffins at the kitchen table, garnering some degree of comfort from the familiar smells and the squirt of hot berries in our mouths.

My friend Elisabeth, a Corsican native whose family foraged off the Mediterranean hillsides, told me about her grandmother's "grass pie"—a lovely baked item filled entirely with wild greens. When Elisabeth forwarded a picture, complete with a list of the foraged items, including wild chard tops and sweet fennel, it resembled an Italian spinach pie covered with a thin pastry dough, rather like something served at Easter but without the ham and eggs.

Back in Brooklyn, inspired by the Corsican grass pie, I collected dandelion greens, common and English plantain, and new field garlic shoots popping up across my neighborhood. Even though these ingredients weren't enough to fill an entire pie, they were a start.

I poured over cookbooks, spread out across my writing desk, and online food websites, such as Epicurious.com. The closest thing I could find to a "grass pie" was spinach and Easter pies—traditional baked dishes popular from Italy and Greece to Lebanon and beyond. Besides eggs and greens, each of them had one other thing in common.

"Ricotta," I murmured, looking up over the open cookbook as my computer went to sleep.

"I want to throw a wild foods brunch," I later told Eli over speakerphone while standing in my kitchen, placing my pie in the heated oven. It was still wet from the egg-wash glaze I'd brushed on.

Eli was back in Brooklyn, packing up for his big move. Even though he was relocating to Boulder the following week, he came over later that afternoon to help me rearrange my furniture so that my two-room apartment—which now smelled rich and cheesy like the savory pie cooling on the kitchen counter—could accommodate eight people.

My apartment was filled with furniture that could expand, accordion-like, throughout the living room. My writing desk, in reality a dining room table, could be expanded to seat a dozen guests; cushy ottomans with removable tops transformed into side tables; a cutting board that fit over the sink extended the kitchen countertop.

"Maybe this is a crazy idea," I said, as we arranged my desk so that it could function as a mini buffet table. I still couldn't visualize more than four people in the apartment. The last time I'd seen that many was when the movers relocated me from Staten Island. And even then, the boxes had practically reached the ceiling and there was barely anyplace to stand.

"If it becomes too much, you can always picnic in the park," Eli said, straightening the tablecloth. "Or someone can always sit on your bed."

While Eli got comfortable on the love seat, I cut into the pie—a test version with a combination of Swiss chard and spinach, plus the grass-fed ricotta and some grated Pecorino Romano. Luckily, Eli wasn't really a vegan and could eat the dairy.

"Hope it's good," I said, sliding a piece onto his plate.

Even though the pie looked beautiful, I was nervous. This was the first time I had baked anything other than a pizza in my oven, and I was uncertain about its capacity to evenly heat food all the way through.

"It's going to be a bit different when I use the real wild greens," I said, sitting down cross-legged on the love seat next to Eli, who was in the middle of taking his first bite.

"It's delicious," Eli said with his mouth full.

I sank my teeth into a forkful. The warm, gooey sensation of grass-fed ricotta and romano cheese married with the bitter edginess of the greens in such a way that I could feel myself almost sighing at the end of every bite.

Eli closed his eyes for a moment, as if he was enjoying the

flavor so much that he couldn't stand to look at anything else. Then, "Can you make this again before I go?"

"Too bad my grandmother can't eat this," I said. Grandma's blood-thinner medication restricted green, leafy vegetables from her diet.

"That's a shame." Eli shook his head before eating another forkful.

"So how's the packing going?" I asked. Our knees were practically touching.

"Almost done," Eli said, swallowing. "I just have a few more boxes."

"I'm going to miss you," I said, putting my plate down. "I can't believe I'm throwing a wild foods brunch and you're not going to be here."

"You should come out to Boulder. It's a great town—everyone's very fit and athletic, and you could do yoga. We could go for hikes and do some Rocky Mountain foraging."

As the light in my living room began to turn golden, hitting the young leaf buds on the trees outside my windows, Eli and I each ate another piece of pie.

A few days later, I received an email from Robert. We hadn't seen each other since the breakup, but I still had a black knapsack of his tucked away in my closet. Since it was so close to my birthday, he suggested that we have dinner together in my neighborhood to celebrate.

Even though I told myself it wasn't a date, I still dressed carefully, in an all-white ensemble: a silk top with a low, flattering neckline and a full cotton skirt that fanned out as I walked.

It was a beautifully warm evening, one of the first of the

season, and I was sitting outside an organic restaurant on the northern edges of Park Slope, reading Euell Gibbons's chapter on Japanese knotweed. I had just discovered the citrusy-tasting plant in Heidi's backyard, and was wondering if I could collect enough to create a rhubarb-like pie.

Robert arrived in his work suit a few minutes later, vaguely out of breath. Not typically relaxed even on a good day, he seemed even stiffer than usual.

"Hey," I said, standing up. In my clogs, we were nearly eye-to-eye.

"Hey there," he said, giving me a kiss on the cheek. He smelled clean, like white soap. "You look great."

I flushed, still finding him attractive. "Here's your bag," I said, handing it to him.

His warm hand lingered over mine a few moments before pulling away.

We were seated in the restaurant's back courtyard, where it was balmy enough to sit through an entire meal without a jacket. We ate the way we used to when we were still a couple—sharing entrees and appetizers, ordering dishes that we knew the other would like. When you haven't seen someone you've known for a while, it's easy to pick up from where you left off, and every movement during dinner, every glance, felt familiar. We sidestepped the issue of whether or not either of us was dating, concentrating instead on our jobs, our families, how much he enjoyed reading my column. I could feel myself getting swept up in the moment, especially when we ordered a slice of peanut butter–chocolate pie to share and our fork tines met.

"Do you ever miss me—miss us, I mean?" I asked, deciding to finally go there.

"Of course, all the time," Robert said. "But I try not to think about it."

"Why not? We had a good relationship," I said. "I didn't break up with you because our relationship was bad—I just needed more."

"I know," he said, looking down at his plate. "And I knew that if I didn't do something, that I would eventually lose you."

"So why didn't you do anything?" I asked, feeling my old frustrations rise in my throat.

Robert didn't say anything. I watched his face harden before he excused himself to go to the restroom.

When it came to certain things like intimacy, Robert always shut his emotions off as if closing the cover of an obscure book, and I had a difficult time reading him.

At the end of the meal, I had calmed down enough to offer him a ride to the train station. "My car's right there," I said, stepping out of the restaurant.

It took only a few minutes to reach his station on Flatbush Avenue, where he could catch the 2 or 3 to Manhattan's Upper West Side.

We sat there for a moment after I turned off the ignition.

"Well, thanks for the ride," Robert finally said, staring ahead out the window. Then, undoing his seat belt, he grabbed his bag.

"Happy birthday," he said, leaning over and kissing me on the mouth.

The kiss was warm and spectacular. Suddenly I was reminded of our very first kiss—an all-encompassing kiss that had us both yearning for more. But instead of being so reminiscent of possibilities, this one was infused with something else.

Before I could open my eyes, Robert broke away and jumped out of the car. I watched him practically run into the train station, his face half in shadow as he descended, not looking back.

I sat in my car awhile, a bit stunned. Then I tried to shake it off—the disappointment, the kiss, whatever it was that I'd been hoping for in seeing him—and turned the ignition back on.

I headed home, taking the road that hugged the park. I kept the windows rolled down, letting the new spring air rifle through my hair and clothing. Back when we first started seeing each other, Robert claimed that he was looking for a relationship that would "go the distance," but six months later, he was having trouble even saying "I love you." Despite my grandmother's warnings and all of the signs that said otherwise, I kept making excuses, holding on to the hope that our love would finally set root and proliferate. Now I knew that it was just another thing that I had to let go of.

Later, back home, the phone rang. My heart raced for a moment, thinking it might be him, but my mother's number appeared on the screen.

"Men are such liars," she said, after I told her what happened. "You don't have to tell *me*."

"It wasn't on purpose," I said, looking at the sliver of moon outside my living room window. "Robert's stuck. If he's lying to anyone, it's to himself."

"All men are *bums*," my mother said, her voice heavy with years of anger and disappointment.

I didn't have the energy to argue, and quickly ended the conversation.

When I was a kid, I had sworn that I would never be like my mother and date the kinds of men that she had—handsome, blue-collar bartenders who resembled my grandfather. Yet somehow, despite our differences, including my moving out of Queens as fast as I could, and the fact that our boyfriends were different both physically and intellectually, I had some-how ended up in nearly the exact same place that she had at my age.

I stood there, watching the moon slowly set behind the rooftops.

Every Chinese New Year, I threw a big celebration for friends, and the February that Robert and I were together was no dif-ferent. I had just stepped out onto a busy Chinatown street, filled with pedestrians rushing to make purchases before the sun went down, my arms heavy with groceries, when a woman carrying a bunch of long-stemmed chrysanthemums the color of egg yolks hurried past. It was then that I saw him, walking toward me, looking a little older and worse for wear, sporting a designer taupe jacket that a family member had given him, the brim of his hat low over his eyes.

"Dad," I said as he approached. Hunched against the cold, with his hands shoved into his pockets, my father looked like someone in a picture of one of New York's huddled masses as he passed. "Stanley!" I said to his retreating back.

Even though we hadn't seen each other in years, I still felt the urge to run after him. I watched the sunlight hitting the back of my father's jacket as he headed up the block, walking like a fast-paced New Yorker through a sea of pedestrians, and I knew that I had to act quickly. My father had what my fam-ily called "Chin" hearing, meaning a singular kind of focus that drowned out other noise, often at the expense of anything else. We all had it—it was how he had kept his practice going for so many years, and how I'd completed a Ph.D. so quickly. Shout-ing would be useless. The only way to catch him was to drop all my bags and dash after him.

I stood there, wavering. It was then that I realized something about the meaning of family: it wasn't just simple biology or genetic inheritance, like resembling someone or having an innate ability that was handed down—it was the investment of time. Family was made up of the people who knew you forever, who stuck by you, despite the arguments and the tension that could build up through the years. Family meant sticking around, even when sometimes you or they just wanted to be left alone.

I knew then that I was tired of running after my father. That period of my life was over.

I watched my father's back grow smaller and smaller before disappearing into the crowd of other coats and scarves like dandelion spores in the city wind.

The morning after my disappointing dinner with Robert, I entered the wide meadow of the park—empty but for two mothers wearing oversize sunglasses and pushing strollers. Although the field was dotted with dandelion and plantain, I was traveling to a higher, more secluded part of the park where the better edibles lay. The air was cool against my face and the hems of my jeans grew wet from brushing up against the morning dew.

I entered the now familiar shady wooded area where it became hilly, which was quiet and damp under the cover of old trees. The air smelled of soil and moisture—and, I thought, climbing across the wood mulch and noting the variety of small green shoots, *kind of like a salad.* I probably wouldn't find any dandelions and plantain here, but I was hoping to collect bunches of tangy field garlic and garlic mustard—enough to feed a group of hungry friends.

As I walked the incline, a pair of chipmunks darted across my path before chasing each other up a gigantic oak tree. Once, Eli and I had found a plate of plantains here, an offering to the most venerable arbor in the area. Another time, while foraging alone, I encountered a homeless person's encampment, complete with the remains of Chinese takeout and several empty forty-ounce beer bottles. I used to be afraid of discovering a dead body here, or getting attacked by an unseen predator with no one around to hear my cries, but those fears dissipated the longer I walked this path and became acquainted with the history, shape, and forms of the various plants that proliferated around me. Today, the base of the oak was covered in a thicket of young shoots and grasses; small pools of water collected within its roots, reflecting back its dark branches and new leaves.

I glanced down, and there at my feet were small garlic mustard rosettes—wee specimens barely taller than my ankles. I got down on my knees and tried to witness one on its own terms: the wavy-edged, scallop-shaped leaves on slender stems that appeared to grow more verdant and deeply veined the longer I looked. Pinching a leaf and crushing it between my fingers, I held it under my nose. It was like the scent of spring mixed with the unmistakable odor of fresh garlic.

I pulled my trowel from my knapsack and started digging. Even though I wasn't as good a digger as Eli, I was learning, carefully moving my trowel around the plant from all sides as he would have done. Garlic mustard had an off-white, edible taproot that was spicy like horseradish, and, luckily for me, it was short and hardy. In just a few moments, I had uprooted the entire plant. I stood up and gave it a good whack, the dirt raining down onto the tops of my sneakers. Farther down the hill, I could see the tubular heads of daffodils and the occasional cluster of purple crocuses.

If I had known when I was still with Robert that I was going to wind up where I was today, thirty-nine and single, I probably would have been even more desperate to make the relationship work—eventually losing even more time, and growing ever angrier and more frustrated.

Instead, as I stood under trees with leaf shoots the color of lime and chartreuse, I wiped the dirt off my hands and ate a small garlic mustard leaf. I headed down the path, my mouth flooded with its spicy green goodness.

When I arrived back home, I drafted the following invite and emailed it out to my friends:

Subject: Spring Foraging Tasting

Yes, it's true: Spring is underway and the greens are delectable and enticing. Please join me and a select cast of foraging-appreciative friends for a spring tasting at my humble Park Slope abode. I will be serving items foraged by my own hands (including contributions from friends).

The Rules:

All dishes will include multiple foraged items; however, not every ingredient will have been foraged (for example, I will not be milking my own grass-fed cow for the ricotta). Each wild edible will be hand-selected by yours truly from some of the sunniest, most elevated pastoral spots in the city, for a truly local, slow-foods affair.

Ingredients most likely to appear on the tasting menu:

- daylily
- field garlic
- garlic mustard
- dandelion

- plantain
- mugwort (aka wild chrysanthemum)

I look forward to seeing you soon!
Ava

At the end of the day, I received several eager confirmations. Sadly, my friend Elisabeth, whose family made that fabulous "grass pie," would be unable to make it.

Sitting at my desk as the sun lowered and bathed my apartment in golden light, I started working on my menu.

This was going to be the tastiest wild foods brunch *ever*.

7

A Wild Foods Brunch

Garlic mustard (*Alliaria petiolata*)

Half an hour before my guests arrived, I had laid out on my dining table the results of a solid week of near-daily foraging. Next to a tossed salad of dandelion greens and garlic mustard, young mugwort shared a giant wooden bowl with fresh field garlic; Japanese knotweed as long as asparagus spears lay near a mass of springy wood sorrel; garlic mustard's ivory roots tangled with the sword-shaped leaves of daylily shoots. Against the living room's whitewashed brick wall, my cornucopia of wild food resembled an artist's still life.

Grabbing oven mitts, I pulled out the star dish that had sparked this whole wild-foods brunch idea in the first place: my version of the Corsican "grass pie"—a Brooklyn-grown wild-greens and ricotta pie. Stuffed with sautéed daylilies, dandelion leaves, and garlic mustard, it was bubbling under a flaky, lattice-top crust that I had just finished making that morning.

I left the dish to cool on the counter, along with two giant bread twists filled with chopped field garlic and daylilies. There were two more pies and several twists in the refrigerator, waiting to be popped into the oven when guests arrived.

I was enjoying the smell of bread-and-buttery goodness filling the apartment, when suddenly the downstairs buzzer rang.

Over the course of the next half hour, my friends arrived: my foraging buddy Deborah—who had shown me on a particularly bitter late-winter morning that wild carrots could grow anywhere, even in the Brooklyn Navy Yard—and her painter husband; my childhood friend Mara and her family, in town from Barcelona; and Heidi, from whose garden I had plucked the wood sorrel and Japanese knotweed, and her engineer boyfriend. Everyone helped themselves to slices of pie. It was thrilling to see them digging into plates full of food, tearing into the twisty breads, and really seeming to enjoy getting to know one another in my cozy quarters.

Deborah's husband, whose artwork reflected the lush plants of his Tasmanian youth, was particularly taken with one weed from the display. "What is this?" Gary asked, studying a stalk with scarlet tinges, which resembled a rather ominous-looking wand.

"Japanese knotweed," I said, crouching down next to him. "Euell Gibbons made it into a kind of rhubarb-tasting pie, but I just like to chew on it or add it to salsa. It's pretty citrusy-sour."

"My housemates waged war on it last summer," Heidi piped in, as a line drawing came alive under Gary's hands. "One of them tried to eradicate it with a makeshift machete."

"It still came back this spring, though," I added, "luckily for us."

"It's banned in England," Heidi said.

"I think they should just eat it," I said. "It's supposedly high in resveratrol."

With its crimson central veins and spiky top leaves, the Japanese knotweed looked like a cross between giant asparagus and the plant in *Little Shop of Horrors*. In fact, I half expected it to start demanding food.

An hour later, I began collecting some of the empty pie tins as the apartment became flooded with late afternoon light. I was considering putting another tray of twists into the oven when my downstairs buzzer rang.

A few moments later, Andy, my editor, came bounding up the stairs. It was my first time meeting Andy, who was lanky, with a shock of curly brown hair and heavy-framed black glasses. He would have looked as much at home in a dusty university library as he did roaming the streets of New York as a metro reporter for the *Times*, which was what he had been for a decade before becoming my editor.

After carefully shaking my hand and assessing the other folks cozily situated on the love seat and random chairs clustered around the close quarters of my living room, Andy leaned against my kitchen counter and dug into the piece of the wild-greens pie I'd handed him.

"What's that?" he asked, nodding toward the greens display. It took me a moment to realize he meant the scalloped-shaped leaves of garlic mustard nestled among the other wild vegetation.

"Garlic mustard," I said, proudly. "I picked it yesterday—it's in the pie and the salad."

"That's not garlic mustard," Andy said without blinking behind his frames.

I may have forgotten to mention that Andy grew up on a former farm in New Jersey, and had been on several tours with Steve Brill. Andy's father could spot the presence of field garlic in the diets of local cows just by tasting their milk. In terms of growing up immersed in nature, Andy had it all over me.

"Yes, it is," I said, trying not to sound too alarmed.

"Garlic mustard has pointier, more triangular-shaped leaves," he said, making a triangle with his fingers. "It grows from a single stalk."

I could feel my face flush. Could I have gotten it wrong? Could Steve Brill have gotten it wrong? Was I now feeding my guests a mysterious and potentially poisonous plant?

"Deborah," I said, grabbing the plant from the table and waving it at her. Deborah was sitting on the couch and entertaining Mara's daughter by pretending she could make a plastic bag appear from out of her hands by sheer magic. "Can you identify this plant?"

Deborah turned the plant in her hands—the rounded leaves were still attached at their base by the white, wizened taproots. "I'm not sure," she said.

"You don't recognize it as garlic mustard?" I asked hopefully. If there were a table I could subtly kick her under, I would have done it.

"I know garlic mustard as having pointed leaves," she said, shrugging.

While I gulped and swiftly tried to extract the plant from her hands as gracefully as possible, stuffing it behind a bowl on the counter so it was out of reach of the other guests, it seemed as if all other conversations in the room had come to a halt.

"But maybe I'm wrong," Deborah said. "It certainly *smells* like garlic mustard."

"I'll look it up later to confirm," I said, turning my back to the countertop. Then, perhaps too brightly, "Anyone want more pie?"

I hoped that putting another dish in the oven would hide my flushed-red face. Even though Andy was standing right next to me, I still couldn't look him in the eye.

Later that evening, after everyone had left and the plates and pie tins were soaking in the sink, I placed the plant that I'd formerly been convinced was garlic mustard on my writing desk. In the lamplight, it looked slightly limp and rather guilty. I filled a shallow bowl with water and tucked its roots in, propping the rest of the plant against the back wall.

The National Parks Service's website had an entire section devoted to alien plants designed in the fashion of a Wild West most-wanted poster. The banner read "Least Wanted" in cowboy-saloon font, suggesting all nonnative plants should be hunted, dead or alive. Even though garlic mustard had arrived in the 1600s through European settlement, it was still an "alien" and not even a naturalized citizen. The site neglected to mention garlic mustard's culinary aspects, as if to discuss any of the plant's usages was to take it out of its category as "weed" (a weed, after all, is inherently *useless*). I looked at the plant on my desk; already, its leaves were beginning to perk up.

According to the website, in its first-year form, *Alliaria peti-olata* grew in rosette clusters with rounded leaves—just like the sample on my desk. In fact, the picture looked exactly like what I had found. I fought the urge to kiss the plant.

As I read further, I discovered that garlic mustard transformed in the later spring into a slender, single-stalked plant with crinkly, heart-shaped leaves (Andy's triangle shapes). I double-checked Steve Brill's book on early spring shoots, and he'd written essentially the same thing about second-year *Alliaria petiolata*. This was my mistake—I'd simply read up on the fall-winter basal rosettes, relying on the information I'd learned last fall, and skipped over the information about what the plant looked like in maturity.

I sat for several minutes comparing the online photos of young garlic mustard with its taller, summertime version and its tiny white cross-shaped flowers. It was hard to believe that in just a few months a plant could change its form so drastically as to be completely unrecognizable.

Andy, Deborah, and I had each been right, though in a way we were all totally wrong. To really know a plant—to truly understand it—you had to be able to identify it in all of its forms: low-to-the-ground winter rosettes, coltish springtime stalks, summer flowerings, and then later, as it went to seed and eventually died back. Even in winter, when the old plant was reduced to its basic shape, like a wizened corpse sticking out of the snow, there were still lessons to be learned.

Botanist Dioscorides, author of *De Materia Medica*, stressed how important it was to know a plant in all of its life cycles: "Now it behooves anyone who desires to be a skillful herbalist to be present when the plants first shoot out of the earth, when they are full grown and when they begin to fade. For he who is only present at the budding of the herb, cannot know it when it is full-grown, nor can he who hath examined a full-grown herb, recognize it when it has only just appeared above ground."

I fingered the garlic mustard in the bowl, now with its stems fully extended and its leaves flush with water. The entire sample was large enough to cover a dinner plate.

I tore off a leaf and chewed, enjoying its tangy goodness. Next month the *Alliaria petiolata* would transform like a teenager into a willowy plant with miniature flowers fit for a maiden's hair. It would taste even sweeter in maturity. While others would be busy ripping it from their gardens, and various divisions of the National Parks Service would attempt to eradicate it from fields and meadows across the country, I envisioned myself wading through giant stands of it, collecting its smooth leaves that when crushed would infuse the air with the scent of garlic.

Wild Greens Pie

This version was inspired by my friend's family Corsican grass pie. Because we don't have the wonderful range of wild edible weeds that they do, I include ricotta and a melting cheese like fontina or Gruyère to round it out. My suggestion is to use grass-fed ricotta if you can get your hands on it, as it really makes a difference in terms of flavor. Depending on the season, I will substitute other wild greens as I find them: dandelion greens, lambsquarters, daylilies, and garlic mustard all work well.

>> **Yields one one-inch pie**

Pie pastry, enough for base and latticework topping

Filling:

2 teaspoons extra virgin olive oil

1 clove of garlic, crushed

1 medium onion, diced

3 cups available wild greens, roughly chopped (daylilies, dandelions, garlic mustard, or lambsquarters)

1 cup spinach, Swiss chard, or store-bought dandelions, roughly chopped

1 cup mustard greens, roughly chopped

$1/2$ teaspoon salt

$1/2$ teaspoon pepper

15-ounce container ricotta cheese

$1/2$ cup grated Pecorino Romano (can substitute Parmesan)

$1/2$ cup grated fontina cheese (or any other good melting cheese you prefer)

$1/2$ cup grated mozzarella cheese

3 large eggs, beaten

1 egg white, optional

1 teaspoon water, optional

1. Preheat oven to 350°F. Press pastry into a 10-inch diameter springform pan. Build pastry up wall of pan at least $1^{1}/_{2}$ inches tall.

2. In a pan over medium flame heat 1 teaspoon of extra virgin olive oil. Add the garlic until lightly browned (3 minutes), and sauté the onions about another 3 minutes. Heat the remaining teaspoon of oil, then mix in the wild and store-bought greens, salt, and pepper. Sauté until all liquid from the greens evaporates, about 3 minutes.

3. Combine the ricotta, romano, fontina, mozzarella, and eggs in a large bowl. Add the wild greens mixture, blending well.

4. Spoon the filling into the pastry-covered pan. Cut the remaining pastry into thin strips and weave into a latticework topping; place over pie, trimming edges. Mix the egg white with the water and brush over pastry, if using. Bake until filling is set in center and browning on top, approximately 40 minutes.

8

Foraging Eyes

Motherwort (*Leonurus cardiaca*)

Eli had a sprawling, geranium-esque plant with long stems and fuzzy leaves growing outside his apartment building in Boulder, Colorado. I spied it as soon as he and I arrived, after stepping out of the car from our hour-long drive from Denver International.

"I wonder if it's edible," I said, bending over the plant, as Eli carried my luggage up the steps to the front door of his building.

I was visiting Eli for four days—crashing at his pad for two evenings, and spending the other nights at a local hotel. Even though it wasn't explicitly discussed, part of the reason I was in town was to see if there was the possibility of something more romantic between us. Many of my friends really liked Eli and were encouraging me to pursue a relationship with him. Even though I had my doubts—what with the long distance and his recent breakup—I figured it was worth a try. A relationship based on a solid friendship seemed like a better possibility than all the speed-dating events in New York City. Though I'd told my grandmother that I was only "visiting a friend" for a few days, I could almost hear her tones of approval ringing in my head.

I followed Eli up the stairs to his second-floor apartment. As he fiddled with his door keys, I studied him from behind. He seemed happier than when I last saw him—chatting away about the cycling club he'd recently joined, the new high-tech bicycle he'd purchased, how he enjoyed biking to work every day. In just a few months, he'd lost ten pounds and everything about him seemed stronger, fitter, and more toned, though I couldn't help noticing that he still sported his stubbly beard, and a hint of sadness remained in those great big Eeyore eyes, even when he smiled.

We entered the apartment—a rental duplex with an open floor plan and a view of the mountains. Even though the furniture was his landlady's and there was very little of "Eli" there, it was comfy and spacious and perhaps most important, ex-girlfriend free.

"I'm really happy here," Eli said, opening a window. "There's good light in the morning and really fresh air.

"By the way, how's your family?" he asked as I sat down at his kitchen table. "How's your grandma?"

"She had a little scare last month and landed in the hospital," I said, toying with a stray packet of salt. "They gave her meds and released her later that day."

"What was the problem?"

"Excess fluid in her legs," I said, shrugging and pushing the salt away. "They say it's something with her heart, but she's ninety-one. Her body's starting to fall apart."

Only a few years before, my grandmother had lost her sister and brother-in-law, who died within days of each other. She had already outlived my grandfather by eleven years and had witnessed the deaths of countless friends and neighbors. Nearly every month, it seemed, there was another notice of funeral arrangements posted in the elevator for neighbors who had passed away. We were losing an entire wartime generation. But for Grandma there was something profound in the loss of her closest sister, Auntie Yuets. These days, she seemed simply tired of being the only one left.

"I'm sorry," Eli said. "Can I get you a glass of water?"

I nodded. "She's back at home now with a full-time aide."

Eli had checked out a few foraging books from the local library, which were sitting in a pile on the table. *Edible and Medicinal Plants of the Rocky Mountains and Neighboring Territories* by Terry Willard; *Edible Wild Plants of the Prairie* by Kelly Kindscher; *Best-Tasting Wild Plants of Colorado and the Rockies* by Cattail Bob Seebeck. I flipped through the line drawings and photographs of sagebrush, angelica, mountain mint, and Jerusalem artichokes. There was no single plant to cure the exhaustion of old age.

"There's a foraging tour tomorrow," Eli said. "If you want to go . . ."

If I were a dog, my ears would have perked up. Instead, I just smiled and said, "Hell, yeah!"

Later that evening, Eli and I lounged on his living room couch after consuming a gigantic vegetable stir-fry. It was like old times again when we used to hang out together—discussing work, family, our exes, how he was acclimating to a new environment. At some point, as we sat on his sofa after dinner, our knees almost touching, I wondered if Eli was going to make a move.

I watched as Eli sat there in the dim lamplight, still smiling at some offhand comment I had made. And then he bounded off the couch, to grab a magazine on outdoorsy things to do in Boulder.

"I looked into renting a tandem bicycle," he said, sitting back down. "But even I realized that might be a bit—"

"—too dorky?" I said, smiling.

"Yeah, too much."

I imagined us riding a two-person bicycle decked out in Victorian outfits—Eli in a suit and bowler hat, myself in a white dress and corset. "Forget it," I said.

When it was time for bed, Eli handed me a set of sheets for the sofa bed. He gave me a friendly hug good night, and I could feel the roughness of his faint beard against the side of my forehead. He smelled comforting and clean—a cross between fresh paint and pine needles.

I listened to Eli's footsteps, with a feeling a little like disappointment, as he headed to his bedroom downstairs.

Brigitte Mars, Boulder's most well-known herbalist and forager, was a slight, Earth-mama type with long pale hair and birdlike movements. On her website, she dressed like a medieval maiden, but in real life, she resembled a hippie version of novelist Mona Simpson, one of my favorite writers. She arrived in a layered bohemian skirt and sandals shortly after Eli and I assembled with about a dozen others in front of a local pharmacy. We were expecting to go on a long hike for Rocky Mountain edibles, but Mars had bad news: even though she'd been leading public tours in the park for years, the Boulder parks department didn't want her conducting them anymore.

"We'll do a walking tour around here instead," she said.

"There are plenty of edibles and medicinals here to show you."

"I thought Boulder would've been more progressive," I said to Eli as we slowly tagged along with the group. "But it's just like New York."

On the Prospect Park tour where Eli and I had first met, a survivalist-type guy dressed in fatigues and carrying a shovel the size of a small child tipped off a park ranger who'd chased us away as we were hunting wild parsnips. While I could understand why the parks didn't want folks willy-nilly digging up plants, I became angry when I later learned that they were planning to raze the entire area to expand the skating rink.

We had walked only a few blocks when Mars stopped in front of a mulched area at the perimeter of a shopping mall. I peered around Eli's yellow windbreaker and saw a familiar-looking plant with deeply grooved fan-shaped leaves.

I nudged Eli. It was the geranium lookalike that was growing outside his building.

"This is malva, or common mallow," Mars said, with the leaves between her fingers. "You can eat the leaves, flowers, and seeds."

"I *knew* it was edible," I whispered.

Mars pushed back a leafy stem and revealed a round "cheese-wheel" seedpod, which resembled a grooved wheel of Brie. "Whenever I take something from a plant, I always thank it," Mars said before chewing.

I searched around for a round pod in the recesses of a plant near my feet. It tasted fresh, and a little like lima beans. The leaves, though, had a fuzzy mouthfeel that made the plant better suited for survival food than for anything I'd want to regularly add to my dinner table. Eli and I looked at each other and shrugged.

We continued walking until we arrived at a residential block with a dead-end road. Mars stopped in front of a tree pit where a lush plant had taken over and was flourishing. The tallest stalk reached my thigh.

"This is motherwort, a calming nervine," she said. "It works on the nervous system."

The leaves were shaped like a lion's tail, and I thought about the Cowardly Lion in *The Wizard of Oz* combing the end of his tail between his paws. I rubbed a leaf between my fingers. The motherwort was less fuzzy than the common mallow and smelled like my grandfather's desk drawer—a repository for curios and odd mementos: pressed handkerchiefs embroidered with someone else's initials, buffalo nickels, an old extracted tooth.

I'd first learned of *Leonurus cardiaca* from a Chinese doctor in Brooklyn, who recommended it for uterine issues like hormonal imbalances and spot bleeding. In Old English, *wort* meant "plant," and I loved the idea of a mothering plant that could aid my feminine issues and calm my nerves. According to David Hoffmann's *The Herbal Handbook,* motherwort was used for menstrual conditions, as a relaxant during menopause, and as a tonic for the heart. Back then, I'd tried the herb in pill form and found it incredibly dry and bitter—I had to drink an entire glass of water to get it down. Because of the taste, I never took it on a regular basis, and so couldn't confirm whether or not it worked. But here it was alive and thriving in the middle of downtown Boulder.

"Like all members of the mint family, motherwort has a square stem," Mars said, gently pushing a leaf aside.

I leaned over a motherwort sprig. The stem felt rough and stiff between my fingers.

"What about the pollution?" someone asked. "Should we really eat something off the street?"

"This is a dead-end residential block," Mars said. "I don't really consider that an issue here."

As Mars led the group away, I lingered behind. Then, I said a little internal thank-you, acknowledging the motherwort, before sampling a leaf. It felt like such a hippie thing to do, but strangely right.

Suddenly I was enveloped in the motherwort's intense bitterness—it was so sharp that my mouth began to water. Instead of feeling calm, I experienced a rise—as if I were on a roller coaster and starting to ascend—before sneezing violently.

"Wow," I said, shaking my head at Eli, who was waiting for me. "That was intense." He turned red from trying not to burst out laughing.

We walked together, lagging behind the others, following Mars around her housing complex. A rather substantial plant had taken over one of the soil beds. "Does anyone recognize this?" Mars asked, as it swayed near her hip. It resembled very tall mint. "You might just want to just observe it first."

A woman with a pageboy haircut raised her hand. "Nettles?"

"*Urtica dioica*. Stinging nettles," Mars said. "High in iron, vitamin K, and calcium—it's great for nursing mothers and boosting breast milk. The stinging action is deactivated when cooked.

You can use it as a hair rinse, and even as a remedy for arthritis and rheumatism. I put it on my eyelids," she added, blinking.

I'd never been stung by a nettle, but I wasn't surprised when someone gasped.

I had nettles tea for the first time last winter back home, and had loved the dense, almost milky flavor, but this was my first time seeing it growing in the wild. With pointed, wavy-edged leaves sprouting from a central stalk, the plant seemed innocuous enough, but for the fine line of thorny hairs running up and down its stem.

Since really knowing a plant means experiencing it in its entirety, I figured that I should feel a nettles' sting at least once—and not just enjoy the benefits dried and collected into a teabag.

While Eli leaned in with his camera, snapping up photographs from under the brim of his baseball cap, I pulled up the sleeve of my sweatshirt and passed the edge of my palm over a section of the plant. I felt nothing more than a tiny prick. I was in the middle of thinking *no sweat*, when the prick started to burn as if someone had lit a match under it.

"Owww," I said, staring at the quickly reddening area, where the almost translucent white stinger, as fine as a hair, was still stuck to my skin. A tiny white bump was starting to rise underneath it. "They weren't kidding when they named it *stinging* nettles."

Eli laughed as I brushed the stinger away and felt the bump under my fingertips.

By the end of the tour, the bump had flattened out into a reddish patch that buzzed like a caffeine high whenever I touched it.

After a late lunch, Eli and I were back hanging out in his living room, listening to NPR. I was planning on taking a yoga class downtown, and until then, was sitting cross-legged in my yoga clothing on Eli's couch, flipping through one of his library foraging books.

Eli sat at the other end, his freckled hands tapping away on his laptop. "You know, I used to give Vera a massage every evening until she fell asleep."

"Really?" I said, reading about chokecherries and prickly pear, not bothering to look up. "Every night?"

"Even after we'd broken up and we were living in separate areas of the apartment, she still wanted a massage. She said it was the only way she could sleep."

"Figures," I said, turning the page. "Some people are *selfish*."

"Do you want a massage before yoga?" Eli asked.

I sat right up, like a cartoon cat that had accidentally stepped on a live wire. Suddenly, I felt jittery and the need to stand.

"We should probably head out," I said. "It takes time to register at a new studio."

Eli just nodded and went to grab his jacket.

I arrived early at the yoga studio, and spent the extra time before class stretching out on a mat, surrounded by mirrors and a clean hardwood floor. As I waited for the others to arrive, I leaned forward onto my outstretched legs, reaching for my ankles, and took a deep breath, trying to sort out my thoughts and feelings.

What was wrong with me? I'd flown all the way out to Boulder, crossing over the Rocky Mountains, just to see if something was going to happen, if Eli would finally make a move. When he did, I bolted.

Eli was my foraging buddy, and despite the different time zone and recent breakup, he was a better bet than most of my previous boyfriends.

So why wasn't I eager to let him touch me?

I sat up into a meditation posture, relaxed half-lotus, with my legs crossed, and noticed all of the thoughts swimming through my head. Sometimes I envisioned goldfish visible through the windows of my eyes, their gills moving along the current of my emotions.

When I was doing my Ph.D. at the University of Southern California, I'd worked with a meditation teacher, the calming Dr. Shing-Shiong Chang, who led a group of graduate students through walking, sitting, and eating meditations. It was Shing-Shiong who first introduced me to the Buddhist concept of monkey mind—the frenetic jumping from one thought and emotion to the next, trying to make meaning of things that often had no meaning, and continuously getting caught up in a cycle of endless thoughts. From the moment on Eli's couch to my arrival in the yoga studio, my own monkey mind had been leaping from bewilderment to rationalizations to accusations.

When our teacher arrived, a gloriously tall and fit young woman with the body of a dancer, I sat up as she led us through a series of full-bodied "oms." Then began the start of an hour and a half of flowing Anusara yoga—incorporating dance-type movements with heart-opening postures. For the first time, I experienced practicing yoga in thinner, mountain air—the conditions under which many world athletes trained. As we transitioned from runners' lunges to warrior poses to extended side angles, turning our torsos toward the ceiling, it felt harder for me to take deep, slow, full breaths, despite the years of yoga I'd been doing back at home. As I shifted, this time binding my arms around my quivering legs and leaning back to face the ceiling again, I was completely focused on syncing my breath with my movement.

Midway through the class, at the point at which I was struggling the most, the music changed to a World Music dance tune—a kind of happy, calypso-inspired song with steel drums—and suddenly our teacher led us through more flowing belly-dance moves, including figure-eight circles with our hips. I followed her example, feeling a little giddy, a little silly, a little *Boulder*, and completely in the moment.

By the end of class, after the last "om," I rolled up my mat and zipped up my sweatshirt, feeling deeply refreshed. It was as if I had gone on a long foraging hike.

I thanked our teacher and stood on line with the other students to put back my props. Both yoga and foraging were forms of moving meditation, like the Buddhist walking and eating practices I'd learned in graduate school. Each was an experiential activity that placed me in what some athletes called "the zone"—whether it was doing triangle pose with my torso parallel to the floor, angled toward my outstretched arm, or hunting for wild edibles. I was only ever able to concentrate on the task at hand, with any extraneous thoughts slipping away like rain down a spout.

I entered the studio's registration-turned-converted-gift-shop area and slipped into my shoes. Eli was at the other side of the room, perusing meditation CDs.

"Hey there," I said, glad to see him.

"How was class?" Eli looked at me with a genuinely open smile. I knew at that moment that everything was going to be fine between us.

"Let's get something to eat," I said, grabbing his arm. "I'm ravenous."

The next few days passed in a flurry of Boulder-immersed activity. We visited the farmers' market, sampling cheeses and local honey and sniffing bars of patchouli and lavender soap; walked the shops along the Pearl Street Mall, where I found wood sorrel growing in a planter under the shade of an ornamental bush; ate at a variety of organic and vegan restaurants; hiked through Chautauqua Park toward the craggy Flatirons. We passed lupine and golden banner in full bloom growing alongside the path, enjoying our walk until a sudden rain forced us to double back toward the car. One morning, we visited the Shambhala Meditation Center, and sat meditating on cushions while a practitioner introduced us to the basic points of Tibetan Buddhism. Before we left, I noticed on the wall that someone had posted a request list for prayers for the sick and ailing. There were already about two dozen names scrawled underneath. I added my grandmother's name in big block letters. Under "Condition," I scribbled: "Wonderfully advanced old age."

Eli helped me check into my hotel, a two-floor sprawler with a car park in the center. The accommodations were lackluster, but the room was perfect for taking the edge off of any need to push or test our friendship, and I was thankful for that.

My last night in Boulder, we came back to my hotel room from a long afternoon barbeque with an old friend of Eli's—a guy he had grown up with from his hometown. While I made small talk with his fiancée and her friend, I could hear Eli laughing and catching up with his buddy at the grill. Eli's laughter was about the only loud thing about him—he even dressed in generally neutral colors, if one made exceptions for the biking gear—and it was a relief to hear him acting so freely.

"I like your friends," I said, plopping down on the perfectly made-up bed later that evening. "It's good that Jason is here."

"It's great having him close by," Eli said, taking out his phone from his pocket and tossing it on the navy bedspread. "He's been introducing me to a lot of his friends here, so I'm meeting more people."

Eli lay down on his side. His elbow created an indentation in the bed, making it easy to lean in closer to him. "A friend of his and I made plans to go biking together—she wants to get more into it and I said I'd help her."

At the mention of "she," I felt a tiny surge of jealousy. But almost as soon as it appeared, it dissipated. "Good," I said. "You need to get out more. It can't just be like when you were living in Brooklyn."

"My life is very different now," Eli said, standing up to head to the bathroom. "I'm much healthier, making better choices for myself. I'm lucky that back then I had you."

As Eli left the room, I lay there staring at the dappled ceiling. It was our last night together and we still hadn't spoken about what was going on between us. Should I be the one to make a move? After all, I was the one who had bolted.

Just then, Eli's phone rang, buzzing and practically jumping across the bedspread next to my head.

"Hey, bay-bee. Pick up, bay-bee. It's *me*," a woman said.

I stared down at Eli's cell phone, as the voice of Eli's ex-girlfriend filled the room. At first I thought Vera was on the line, amped up on speakerphone, and that she could hear—perhaps even *see*—me. But I soon realized that this was Eli's specialized ring-tone for her.

"Hey bay-bee . . . It's *me* . . ."

Even though she was from California, Vera sounded familiar, like one of my cousins from Long Island.

The ring tone seemed endless as I scrambled to find the button to silence it. In my head, I considered these options: tossing the phone out the window, smothering it with a pillow, smashing it against the wall. Finally, after several successive "Hey, bay-bee. Pick up, bay-bee. It's *me*" cycles, the call went to voicemail.

When Eli finally emerged from the bathroom, I was sitting in a silent room.

For some reason I couldn't quite put my finger on, I was fuming. "Your phone went off," I said darkly.

Eli just stood by the bed and blinked.

"It was *Vera*," I said.

"I'll call her back later."

"Why are you still talking to her—and why do you still have that ring tone on your phone?" I frowned. "It's really annoying."

"She put it on there a long time ago," he said, sitting down on the edge of the bed. "I never got around to changing it."

"How often do you guys talk?"

"Every day."

"Are you serious?" I said, trying to keep my facial expressions neutral, but failing.

"She calls me—I don't call her."

"But you're not together anymore," I said. "She should call someone else."

Eli, resembling a dejected kid, looked away.

All this time, I'd assumed that he had made a clean break, but there it was. Despite the distance, Vera was still calling him every day, and despite his having called it quits several months before, he was still there for her.

I reached for the TV remote control. At that moment, even watching the local news seemed better than to continue talking about Vera. We spent the next hour flipping through the channels until Eli sat up from the bed and prepared to go home.

After we hugged good-bye, I watched him walk down the stairs. The phone created a bulge in his back pocket that was visible all the way to the car.

The next morning, Eli picked me up at the hotel, where my bags were packed and ready. After breakfast, we still had time for a hike before my flight back to New York, and so we headed out for a local park on the edge of town.

I was still keenly interested in what we might be able to find in the way of Rocky Mountain edibles, and wanted to apply the new knowledge we'd learned from Brigitte Mars. As we walked along a winding path that hugged a lively creek, I kept an eye out for anything identifiable.

"I was thinking about you after you left," I said. It was warm but slightly overcast, and as we walked farther away from where the car was parked, I could see slate-blue mountains in the distance. "Sorry I was so negative last night."

"I guess I'm still a little tender since the breakup," Eli said. I could barely see his expression under his baseball cap and five o'clock shadow. Only his mouth moved. "I don't think I'm ready to date just yet."

We continued walking, passed only by the occasional jogger and cyclist. Eli had been with Vera a long time—I could only imagine how he felt. I'd been with Robert only a year, but at our age, relationships were harder to get over than when we were younger.

"I can't tell you what to do, but if she's calling you every day and you take her phone calls, it's going to be harder to move on," I said, reaching for my sunglasses. "And when you are ready, it may affect your ability to be with someone else."

"I can't stop her from calling—she just calls."

"There's nothing that says that you have to talk to her," I said. "You've broken up—you don't owe her anything."

Eli just looked forward along the path, not saying anything.

"You're two thousand miles away and she's still trying to hold on. What was it that your therapist in New York said, about your needing to do things for yourself?" I asked.

"Yeah, you're right," Eli said. "I have to take care of myself before I can be there for anyone else."

As we walked, I noticed slight movements across the prairie. It was only when we paused that I saw hundreds of bouncy little prairie dogs, congregating around small burrow openings. In numerous mounds all across the field, clusters of them were sniffing the air, darting toward one another, or standing stock-still with their tails extended. Perhaps they were sensing us, as suddenly, several began barking, until we were surrounded by a cacophony of calls.

"They're hilarious!" Eli said, taking out his camera.

As Eli crouched down, smiling and focusing his lens on the nearest group, I noticed among the spiny sow thistle and gnarled trunks of old trees a lush, knee-height plant flourishing across the plain. Upon closer inspection, I realized it was motherwort, the plant that we had seen growing on Brigitte Mars's block. Here, the *Leonurus cardiaca* was alive and thriving in giant bunches—even outnumbering the prairie dogs Eli was so amused by.

I stepped a yard off the path, mindful of keeping my distance from any of the alert little animals, and studied a patch as large across as my arm. All around the tall central plant were smaller patches of motherwort, and I realized that I was standing over the "mother." Mars had taught us to respect the mother—the gift that kept on giving—so I left it alone and inspected one of the daughter plants instead, breaking off a leaf near the top, where smaller leaves had already started to form. "Thank you," I whispered.

The motherwort was extremely bitter and sharp, and just as I'd done on Mars's block, I sneezed suddenly and loudly—sparking another chorus of alarmed barking from the prairie dogs.

I held out a young leaf to Eli. "Try it—it's really strong."

Eli put it in his mouth, and then chewed for a second before spitting it out onto the ground.

"Wow," he said, shaking his head.

I couldn't stop laughing, looking at Eli's expression as he wiped his bottom lip. "I *told* you it was strong."

As we continued our walk along the winding path between the rushing river and the embankment, it felt as though everything had changed. Even the frenetic movements of the prairie dogs seemed slower, more methodical. Suddenly, I loved the feeling of the overcast light on my face and hands. I loved Boulder. I loved motherwort. I loved Eli.

"Quick, take a picture," I said, jumping off the path again and trying to embrace a springy patch of motherwort that reached my thighs.

I put my face into the motherwort and nuzzled it. I could feel the entire plant photosynthesizing under the open prairie sky and pouring the oxygen straight into my nostrils.

"You nut!" Eli said, laughing, and pulling his camera from his pocket.

As I crouched there, smiling up at him, happy about my find, I realized that there was a proper timing and situation for everything. Some things I couldn't force, and neither could he. Looking at Eli with soft, foraging eyes, as he leaned forward on bent knees and snapped a picture of me hovering over the *Leonurus cardiaca* with his digital camera, I could see that he existed on his own terms. He wasn't there to be pushed or prodded or molded into what I, or anyone else, including Vera, might want him to be. Eli was Eli. He couldn't make himself fall out of love with Vera, just as I couldn't make myself fall in love with him.

I posed, smiling and breathing in the Rocky Mountain air. Everything around us from the brown earth, dappled with weeds and medicinal herbs, to the bouncing prairie dogs darting from burrow to burrow seemed edged with a brightness and clarity I had never before noticed. I vowed at that moment to always keep my eyesight keen—whether I was searching for wild edibles or involved in a relationship, any relationship. No more daydreaming or projections, no more forcing a square peg into a circle, no more waiting around for something that wasn't going to happen.

Here I was, two time zones and two thousand miles away from home, still carrying with me all of my old issues. The only difference, as I sat surrounded by the motherwort waving in the wind—its fat, sun-soaked leaves getting caught in my hair and clothing—was that now it was getting easier to appreciate the really, really good things all around me.

While Eli took another picture, I ate another motherwort leaf. This time I didn't sneeze.

Motherwort, Drying Techniques

Herbs like motherwort dry quite well, and if I'm traveling shortly after collecting it and I do not have the time (or the equipment available) to make an herbal tincture, then drying it is the way to go. (Note: This technique works best if it isn't a terribly humid or rainy day).

1. Make sure your plant parts, in this case the leaves, are clean. Discard any that are yellowed or full of holes.

2. Place them evenly on a mesh screen (I sometimes use a steamer rack from my wok, or a mesh splatter screen). Make sure the leaves are evenly spaced, with no overlap. You want the plant to dry thoroughly without molding.

3. Place the screen on an elevated surface, so that it gets adequate air circulation underneath as well as on top. I sometimes place the screen on top of two stacks of books spaced about a foot apart. Allow to dry for 24 hours.

4. The next day, turn the leaves over to air-dry the other side.

5. Continue to monitor over the course of the next two days, turning the leaves as necessary, until they are completely dry.

Summer

9

The Mother Borough

Mulberries (*Morus rubra, M. alba*)

B y the time I returned home, the city had transformed into the lushness of early summer. Cafés and restaurants threw open their patio doors, and I could hear the clink of silverware against dishes as I walked down my block, on the hunt for violet leaves and mature garlic mustard. My neighborhood was resplendent with natural treasures: After a sudden rainstorm, I discovered tiny, brown-capped mushrooms that disintegrated into inky pools at the slightest touch of my finger. A giant reishi mushroom blooming on the trunk of a London plane tree. The notched shoots of Asiatic dayflower, growing in front of my stoop under a bicycle wheel.

For my column, I wandered through parking lots and various residents' backyards, including the patio vegetable garden of one of our readers to identify a bit of common mallow growing wild there. I found a cacophony of violets growing outside a dry cleaner and then another in front of an old abandoned school on the border of neighboring Bedford-Stuyvesant. Once, I nearly stepped on the rotting carcass of a rat, trying to get a good shot of violet flowers, their bearded white and purple heads dipping on delicate stems, while behind me a car drove by blasting music so loud that the bass rattled its back windows.

In between the foraging and writing, I signed up for more classes, including an introductory herbal medicine course. I soon learned that the knowledge my grandfather imparted to me as a child, coupled with my own newfound foraging habits, had laid the foundation for my understanding of botanical medicinals. Each week, I squeezed into a tiny classroom with about eight other students at the Third Root Community Health Center in Ditmas Park, Brooklyn, learning about the benefits of herbs like echinacea, astragalus, and elecampane. I told my classmates about my grandfather's soups and his use of various mushrooms and roots, as well as my latest wild reishi discovery, as we sat making herbal tinctures—tearing *Ganoderma lucidum* into small strips or bruising pine needles before forcing them into empty baby-food jars with vodka solutions. Then we vigorously attempted to shake the medicine into existence.

I also enrolled in a cooking class at a popular culinary school in the Flatiron District. ("I like the sound of that!" said my grandmother with some of her old exuberance.) As I tried my hand at braising sinewy cuts of meat, reduction sauces, and cooking with a variety of traditional ingredients, I once again felt the influence of Grandpa's palate and my own newfound foraging habits. One class, I brought in some daylily blossoms gathered from a friend's backyard, and after completing my portion of the class assignment, sautéed the *Hemerocallis fulva* in Plugrá butter.

I spent so much time either in classes or rooting around the ground, inspecting the variety of edible plant life growing around my neighborhood, that the morning I received an email message from my editor, Andy, informing me that we were in the height of mulberry season and that I should find a *Morus* tree to profile, I was almost profoundly, distractingly disturbed.

"Where the hell am I going to find a mulberry tree?" I murmured to myself, grabbing all of my foraging books from off the bookshelves. I wasn't even certain what a mulberry looked like.

I poured over my books, hoping to bone up on my tree identification. According to Gibbons in *Stalking*, there are two different kinds of mulberry trees that grow throughout the country, the native red mulberry (*Morus rubra*) and the Chinese white mulberry (*Morus alba*); the latter were imported from China in the 1800s to support a burgeoning silk industry. Though it eventually went bust (apparently, sericulture was extremely labor intensive and difficult to reproduce in the United States), the white mulberry flourished, hybridizing with the native red, and could now be found across the country. Both varieties—which weren't bushes as the children's song purported—have characteristically varied leaf shapes with different numbers of lobes all within the same branch. Finding one was going to be even harder than I'd anticipated.

I was reading up on the fruit—not a true berry as the name implied, but an aggregate fruit cluster, like a raspberry or blackberry—when the phone rang.

It was my mother.

"Grandma's in the hospital," she said. "She's been transferred out of the ER to a room."

"What happened?" I asked, standing up from my desk so

fast that the chair legs scraped loudly across the wood floor. The week before, she'd fallen asleep at the kitchen table and blackened her eye. "Where is she?"

"Her legs blew up and she was in a great deal of pain," Mom said. "I don't know the room number."

"All right, I'm heading over."

I was still dressed in my at-home writing outfit—a man's shirt and yoga pants that had lost their stretch—and tried putting on real clothing while simultaneously dialing the hospital. Outside my window, squirrels were foraging along the branches of my downstairs neighbor's tree.

When a receptionist finally picked up, she connected me to my grandmother's room. But the phone just kept ringing and ringing.

Just as I was grabbing my keys, I heard noises at my window that sounded like swimmers jumping off a diving board. The squirrels had landed onto my fire escape and were racing up the ladder toward the roof. I didn't know where they were going in such a hurry, but their anxious scrambling reminded me of the Boulder prairie dogs living among the motherwort.

Leonurus cardiaca. If there was ever a time I needed something to calm my nerves, it was now. I grabbed the dried leaves I'd brought from Colorado, stored in the cupboard with a now growing collection of dried fungi and herbal tinctures. Then I ran out of the apartment with my overnight bag and bounded down the stairs.

Grandma was lying in a hospital bed, an IV in her arm, when I arrived. When I touched her hand it was cold.

"Hi, Grams," I said, thankful when she opened her eyes. "How're you feeling?"

"Whatcha doing here?" she said. "Where's Laura?"

"She's coming," I said, lying. I had no idea where my mother was. "You need anything?"

She shook her head. "I'm glad you're here," she said. Then, closing her eyes, "I hope that I don't have to stay here long."

The room was cold and brightly lit, and I was glad that I'd brought my jacket. I watched her lying there until her breathing was slow and rhythmic, and eventually she fell asleep. In a little while, the rest of the family arrived—first my mother, then my uncle and cousins. Everyone was talking loudly and laughing to try to lighten up the mood, and Grandma just lay there, looking like the matriarch she was, only a little more diminished.

I didn't feel like talking either, so I just sat in a chair, watching her, trying to breathe into the spot in my chest where I held my deepest fears, attempting to remember her the way she was when I was still growing up and trying to soak up everything she'd taught me.

For the next few days, my grandmother stayed in the hospital, while I slept at her apartment. Each day, I walked through the back end of her neighborhood, through the residential side streets with the attached homes, past a small extension of Kissena Park across from the Queens Botanical Gardens, and up the slight hill toward the hospital. It was the same hospital where my grandfather had been taken when he was dying. It was also the hospital where I had been born.

When I arrived that morning, my mom was already there, sitting in a chair next to Gram's bedside. Grandma was dozing.

"How's she doing?" I said, idling up to the bed.

A vein in my mother's temple throbbed. Despite the years, Mom was still attractive—just an older, fuller version of her

Miss Chinatown self in supportive shoes. Her eyes were lined with the same brand of black liquid liner that she used when I was a kid. *Maybelline eyes.* "They may discharge her today, if all goes well," she said.

I felt a flood of relief as I looked down at my grandmother, her head tilted slightly away from me toward the curtain separating her side of the room.

"It's a good thing we brought her to the hospital," my mother said, lowering her voice. "They found a blood clot in her leg that could have gone straight to her heart."

"But isn't she on anticoagulant meds?" I asked, almost accusatorily. That was the reason why she couldn't eat my wild greens pies or any other green leafy vegetable I had found. "That wasn't supposed to happen."

My mother shrugged. "Luckily, they caught it and everything else checks out fine. Perhaps she'll be home for her birthday."

Goddamnit, I thought, as my grandmother suddenly stirred.

While my mother went to the bathroom, I leaned over Grandma. "They think you may be able to go home today," I said, touching the coarse whiteness of her hair.

"I hope so," she said, wincing, her hand on her stomach. I knew that her legs were swollen under the sheet. "Why does it still hurt?"

"I don't know," I said.

When I was little and we were still living with my grandparents, anytime I fell or stumbled or hurt myself, my grandmother would distract me from my pain with something simple: pots and pans, a stuffed animal, a soft cloth. Sometimes, if I stubbed my toe on furniture or simply tripped over the rug, either my grandmother or mother would hit the offending object and deem it *bad*.

But here in the cold hospital room, there were no household objects or soft cloths to distract her. Only the advancement of old age, and her own rapidly deteriorating body.

I remembered something from one of our old conversations when I was a kid and Grandma was my near-sighted hero. "You know, I think you're very brave," I said. "*You* can withstand pain greater than I can."

"What do you mean?" she said, closing her eyes.

"You had three babies," I said. "And remember what you told me when I was little?"

With her eyes firmly shut behind her glasses, my grandmother shook her head.

"You said that giving birth really hurts," I said slowly, trying to precisely recall her words. "But once you see that cute little baby, you forget all about the pain."

A smile fluttered across my grandmother's face, and for a brief moment she was glorious as she remembered the moments of her children's births—Kenny, Wesley, and finally my mother. They were all born in different parts of the country, from Washington state to D.C. to New York, but I could tell that each birth was special to her.

"Oh yes," Grandma breathed, still smiling as she fell back to sleep.

A few days later, we celebrated my grandmother's ninety-second birthday back home at her apartment. It was just a small group of us, and the tray tables and chairs lay folded and propped up against a wall. Mom was chattering on about how she'd gotten a deal on a new ring by selling an old one, the new ring glittering on her finger.

Although my mom nearly always claimed that she was

broke, there was always another new piece to admire. It took years for me to understand just how much jewelry made her feel validated. *I don't need a man*, she would tell me, *I can buy myself diamonds.*

Mom did the dishes, talking in a voice louder than the running water to my grandmother about some new sale. I turned on the deaf ears, watching Grandma, who just sat at the kitchen table, looking small and wistful with her hearing aids in, her arthritic hands folded. Usually she nodded and commented and assessed everything that my mother did—Mom's latest purchases, her quibbling at her job with so-and-so—so that I could remain blissfully free of it and didn't need to say anything at all.

What will it be like when she's gone? What kind of family life will we have? I didn't want to think about it.

I watered the plants, which were wilting from neglect, picking out the dead, withered leaves. There had been no babies that year, only the monstrous spider mothers hanging from the ceiling, soaking in the summer sunlight from the windows. I could hear the teenagers playing basketball below. The bouncing of the ball against the court. The occasional cheer whenever someone made a shot.

After the dishes, my mother read aloud each of Grandma's birthday cards. I climbed down from the plants and sat at the table. Grandma's hair was so thin and fluffy that I could see through it to the back wall with the row of framed photographs of her great-grandchildren—great-grandsons dressed up in button-down shirts and V-neck sweaters, from babies to preschoolers, smiling wide for the camera. Next to them, she'd taped a copy of one of my columns with my picture, taken at a high school reunion.

Even though Mom had several more cards to go, Grandma seemed genuinely distracted, as if she were already somewhere else.

I was just waking up from a nap on the sofa when I heard my mother say my name. She was staring at me from the kitchen table, along with my uncle and my grandmother's aide, Daphne.

"Daphne needs to take the night off and we want you to stay with Grandma that weekend," my mom said.

"Okay," I said, rubbing my eyes.

"And then I'm having foot surgery, so you'll come over to my place and take care of me."

Hold on a minute. I looked over and everyone was staring at me, except for Grandma, who had that faraway look on her face again, regarding something through the terrace door.

"When is this?"

"The week after next—the day after you take care of Grandma."

"I have to check my calendar," I said, stalling. "I might have class that night."

"Why'd you offer to help, then?" my mother said, her tone suddenly harsh. Whenever I didn't agree with her right away, she always sounded angry.

"I need to check my calendar and then I'll let you know." I sat up and went to the bathroom—the easiest way to make an exit.

I was in my car an hour later, searching for a parking spot in now-familiar Fort Greene, close to the train station. If I didn't find one fast, I was going to be late meeting my date near Union Square in Manhattan. As I passed the park, home of field garlic and evergreens, I thought about my looming mulberry deadline. In between dashing off to Flushing from Brooklyn to take care of family members, when was I supposed to find a mulberry—a tree that had a myriad of leaf shapes *even on the same branch*?

I spied a parking spot and slowed down, putting on my blinkers.

On the street, I rushed toward the train station in my clogs, the subway only a few blocks away. I was trying not to worry about Grandma and her hospitalization, and my mom's *and then you'll take care of me*, but the pressure, plus my deadline, was permeating my thoughts like spring pollen, even as I hurried past the mom-and-pop stores on DeKalb Avenue. Why did my mother have the expectation that I would just drop everything and play nurse to everyone? Why was everything about *her*? I could feel my face getting red with anger as I adjusted my bag and walked even faster.

Ever since I was a kid, I had to navigate my mother. Nearly everything about her was louder and larger than life—her vivacious laughter, her beauty, her sense of style and taste in men. Even her moods swung wildly, like thunderstorms in August. She could be loving one moment—grabbing me into her arms and hugging me tight, saying that I would always be her *baby* even when I was grown-up—to cold and angry and resentful the next, sometimes cursing me and men and life all in the same breath.

Because she was the one who stayed, as a kid I clung to her desperately like floating debris in a storm, defending her to my grandparents, refusing to give up on her. When my grandparents criticized the way she was raising me, I spoke up. *I was fine. I did well in school. I didn't need religious instruction.*

When Mom made mistakes, I covered them up. I didn't tell anyone about the sneaking away at night so that she could party with friends. This was the 1970s, and the rhetoric of the day revolved around a woman's independence. *Everyone needs time away from the kids,* I insisted, parroting my grandmother; *she's young and beautiful, she should have a good time.* When Mom sold our old Chevy Nova and replaced it with a two-seater sports car, I didn't complain, even though it was often her excuse for leaving me behind. *There's no room for both you and _____.*

I did all of this as a child, until one day, something inside me snapped shut. Perhaps it was puberty. Perhaps it was her then boyfriend, a baby-faced bartender who lived with his parents and was closer to my age than to hers. Perhaps it was just the years of living so close to the impulsive mood swings and rejections.

In the face of her loudness, her anger at my father, and even her intermittent laughter, which sometimes cascaded around us in the rare, beautiful moments she was truly happy, I often felt like I was disappearing. So I learned to erect walls of my own—crawling inside nests of books, school, and later the arms of boys who claimed that they loved me.

It was only when I moved out—suddenly, after a fight, when I was a college sophomore, writing her an eight-page letter with all of my grievances—that I expressed all the pain and anger I'd been harboring for years, buried deep inside me for fear that she'd leave, too. Everything came pouring out. Those nights leaving me home alone as a child. My resentment over her formidable rage, which squelched any attempts I made to address my own feelings. *If you don't like it,* she often screamed, while I ran into my bedroom, *then you can go live with your father.* I taped the handwritten letter to my bedroom door and left.

We didn't talk to each other for three months, and in that time, Grandma took the place of Mother in my heart: She was the one who met all my boyfriends; she lent me money; she was the recipient of all my love and cooking and phone calls, even when I was thousands of miles away in graduate school. When I taught my creative writing classes, I talked about the lessons Grandma had given me. Mom moved down in status to something like *older sister*, and our relationship had remained that way ever since.

Only now, we were losing my grandmother, and who was going to fill in that spot in both of our hearts?

I was passing a slow-moving elderly woman with shopping bags in both arms and a bald guy smoking outside a convenience store plastered with advertisements for beer, when I took a misstep. I stumbled, and a shooting pain ran up my left ankle toward my calf. Suddenly, I was falling toward the concrete as my ankle gave way underneath me. I put my hands out, bracing for a fall.

Somehow I righted myself so quickly that no one even noticed. The woman continued walking and the smoker finished his cigarette, tossing the butt out into the gutter. But when I tentatively put weight down on my left foot, I felt that shooting pain again in my now hot-and-tender ankle.

"Ow-ee!" I said, feeling the blood rushing toward the inflamed joint.

The last time I'd injured that ankle was when my grandfather died. I twisted it while taking a wrong step onto a subway platform. It took several months for the swelling in my ankle to fully subside, and it was never the same again.

I paused for a moment, looking at my rapidly swelling ankle. I could stop now, and head back to my car, or I could travel into the city and get my date to help me purchase an Ace bandage (there was a pharmacy by the subway on the other side). I looked back down the avenue, in the direction of my car, which seemed so far away—even farther than the train station. Even if I turned back, I knew I couldn't drive my manual-transmission clutch with my ankle being so swollen.

Since it was so late, I decided to head into the city. At least in the movie theater, I figured, I could sit down with my ankle elevated.

A few days later, I sat in front of my computer with my Ace-bandaged ankle propped up on a chair as I filed a call for mulberry trees.

> Mulberry tree lovers: Do you have a favorite *Morus rubra* or *alba* tree in the neighborhood? The Urban Forager would love to profile it in an upcoming posting. Drop us a line with your email-contact info. —*AVA CHIN*

Shortly after it went up, one reader posted a comment about his distain for the trees—mainly based on the abundant messiness of the fruit. "My favorite one is the one that was chopped up and taken away out of my old backyard. That thing used to rain mulberries down into a rotting swamp of mulberry muck unless I shoveled it (literally) at least once a week," wrote *BGGB*.

I sighed, hoping someone would come through with an actual tree for us to profile, when the phone rang. It was my mother.

"It's Grandma," she said, her voice tight and clipped in a way that made me stop looking at my computer screen. "She's in the emergency room."

I immediately sat up in my chair. "What? Again?"

"We're leaving the hospital now—to make arrangements."

I felt that cold sensation of going numb and not feeling altogether there, like when I received the phone call that my grandfather died.

I looked down at my left ankle. Swollen to the size of a tennis ball, again.

When I arrived at the emergency room, Grandma was in a hospital bed, mumbling to herself, a thin wraparound curtain the only thing separating her from the other patients on either side. She was lying in the half-light attached to an IV drip and a heart monitor, the electronic beeps mixing with the constant noise of patients being wheeled in and out, and hospital staff yelling out greetings and warnings.

"Grandma, it's me," I said, stroking her hair. "I'm here," I said, a little more loudly than before.

As I leaned forward, my ankle began throbbing. I would have killed for a chair, but even if I found one, there wasn't enough room to wedge it between her bed and the other patients.

A nurse appeared at the curtain. "Are you the daughter?" she asked, checking my grandmother's monitor. "Did the family make a decision about the DNR?"

"Granddaughter," I said. "What's that?"

"A Do Not Resuscitate order," she said. "Otherwise we'll do everything we can to keep her alive."

"Oh," I said, not wanting to cry. "I'll ask my mother."

I got on my cell phone as soon as she left, even though calls were forbidden.

My mother picked up on the first ring.

"They asked me about a DNR," I whispered. "I didn't know what to tell them."

"We're going to sign it."

My heart stopped a little as I looked down at my grandmother, still moaning in pain.

"I'll come over as soon as I can," my mother said before hanging up.

I was fighting back tears as I leaned over my grandmother's bed. "Mom is on her way."

My grandmother opened her eyes and blinked a few times behind her glasses, before focusing her good eye on me. She mumbled something incomprehensible.

"I can't hear you," I said.

"Always," she said, a little more clearly, "always remember me and Grandpa."

"I will," I said, as tears began welling up in my eyes.

Goddamnit, I thought, fighting the tears. I was about to lose the only remaining person who'd stood by me my entire life and loved me unconditionally. Why did it have to be *her*?

I watched as the monitor by her bed jumped from 43 to 70, then down to 30. When it dipped to zero, I felt my breath catch and for a few heart-stopping seconds I panicked, wanting to thump on her chest until her heart started beating again. But suddenly it jumped back up to 42, and I could breathe.

My grandmother turned to me and said, "I love you."

"I love you, too, Grandma."

"You were always so good—the best one, the very best one. You always came back to me."

I could barely see her through the blur of my tears, but I could hear her voice, clearly now, over the sounds of her machine, the numbers changing yet again.

"I'm so proud of you—of the person you've become. Grandpa and I always wanted you to get a good education," she said, drifting off. "I'm sorry."

At first, I didn't know what she was apologizing for—then I

remembered: When I was seventeen, my grandfather ran up a huge gambling debt, and it was Grandma who had bailed him out. Since there was no money to send me away to college, I attended CUNY, the same system that now employed me.

"Please don't apologize," I said, squeezing her hand and continuing to stroke her hair. "It all turned out fine. I'm fine."

"You're the only one who's not married—" she continued.

"I'm sorry, Grandma," I said, crying so hard that I found it difficult to breathe. "I'm so sorry." Suddenly, I was consumed with grief and guilt and feeling like a complete failure.

"I have five granddaughters," she said, oblivious to me, or the beeping of her monitor.

I wiped away my tears and held her hand, wanting to break her machine.

"I've lived a long happy, happy life. A happy, happy life."

She paused, the numbers on her monitor shifting again. I looked instead into the inky dilation of her eyes.

"But it's time for me to go now—I have to go."

"Okay, you go," I said, trying to smile. "We'll be all right, I promise. The family will be fine. You do what you have to do. I'll be here for you."

"Okay, bye-bye," she said. She grabbed at the IV in her arm, and before I could react, pulled it out, so that it dangled over the side of the bed like a pen attached to a clipboard.

My tear ducts were smarting as I watched, half in awe, half in dismay, as she then started pulling at the cords at her chest under the hospital gown. She was having trouble with the last ones.

I didn't know what to do. Helping her would be killing her, but not helping was to prolong the agony and stand in the way of a clean, conscious break. She was so clear and so strong about it. Why couldn't I be?

I looked around at the whirl of activity in the ER—all the nurses and residents and sick patients—but no one was watching us or paying any attention.

As she struggled with the cords and tape, I did the only thing I could think of—I pulled the sheet up over my grandmother's chest and covered up her moving hands. For a few moments, her movements were hard and jerky under the sheet, before she finally broke free of all the wires, and relaxed with a sigh.

I'd never witnessed death this close before. Everything I'd watched on television showed a speedy ending. I kind of expected my grandmother to collapse with a dramatic dip of the head or a jerk of the shoulder. Instead, she just kept lying there breathing shallowly, while the nurses tended their stations, making their rounds, and the orderlies transferred patients in and out of the area.

I was standing there, babying my bad ankle and shifting my weight onto my good one, wondering which moment would be her last.

For several minutes, there was just the usual din of ER activity and the beeping of her machine. The intermittent numbers, jumping higher, then lower, sometimes staying in the middle.

I was holding her hand and zoning out when Grandma, who was staring at the ceiling, suddenly gasped.

She looked at me, as if she was struggling to recall my name. Then she simply said, "Granddaughter."

Then, she looked back up at the ceiling again and murmured, "It's so beautiful."

I looked up at the hospital ceiling. I tried to envision what she was seeing—a celestial mass of lights? A glowing doorway? A swirling, beckoning tunnel? The navel of the universe?

But instead of lights and swimming angels, all I could see

was the crummy, crumbling synthetic white soundproofing of the ceiling through the blur of my own tears.

⁓

I lost all track of time in the noise and continual din of the emergency room. The rotation of the staff. Patients being wheeled in and out. Someone calling out for help. My own throbbing ankle.

I looked at the time on my cell phone. I'd been in the ER for three hours.

Suddenly, a nurse appeared at the curtain.

"What's this?" she said, quickly surmising that the IV was out. She clucked at my grandmother, as if she were dealing with a child, "What did you do?"

She stuck the needle back into her forearm and chastised her.

I wanted to protest, *Leave her alone—this is what she wanted—she knew what she was doing.*

But it was pointless. Even though I had often felt like my grandparents' fourth and last child, I had never felt so helpless. I was a granddaughter with no authority. I didn't have the power to make her well—no matter what medicinal plants or mushrooms I could find in the wild—and I couldn't sign a stupid paper that would set her free.

I stood there as my grandmother opened her eyes and watched the nurse reattach all of the cords to her chest.

The next day, she was nonverbal, eyes closed, and on a respirator. She was able to squeeze my hand or move her foot in response when I whispered in her ear how much we loved her. How proud I was of her. How when it was time, *she should just let go*.

On Sunday, we found her laid out on her bed immobile, her

extremities growing colder, as the IV fluid circulated throughout her body.

Her hand was wet as I held it, clear fluid seeping out of the holes from where the staff had stuck her with needles.

"Let's wipe her up," my mother said, sopping it up with a napkin.

Early the next morning, we received the phone call that my grandmother had passed away. It suddenly seemed too bright in the living room where I'd just been sleeping. *Grandma is dead. She's finally passed away.* I pulled on my skirt, which I'd left in a pile on the floor from the night before. I felt like I was moving through water.

Forty-five minutes later, my mother and I were in the car, driving toward the hospital.

"Her being gone is going to be weird for you," I said, half hoping this would create an opening for us to talk about how it would be for me, too.

"I know," she said, driving uncharacteristically slowly. "I usually pick her up every Saturday for lunch and to go shopping."

She didn't say anything more, just drove past the familiar landmarks from my childhood. The savings bank with the white steeple. The run-down movie theater. The old two-room library where I'd checked out my first books. Unlike me, who'd escaped to Brooklyn as soon as I could afford it, and then eventually three thousand miles across the country, my mother had never lived less than five miles away from my grandparents.

Grandma and my mother had always been close. Mom was her baby daughter, the little beauty whom everyone, even strangers, wanted to hold. There was a picture of my mother from back then, in a white dress, her hair carefully rendered by my grandmother into tight curls framing her round face. Baby Mom was looking into the camera with her eyebrows furrowed, wearing an expression so open and earnest that it hurt every time I saw it. Even though she was now an aging boomer, a regular card-carrying member of the AARP, Grandma had regarded Mom as if she were still her little girl in full bloom, Miss Chinatown, with a bevy of weekend suitors.

Your mother loves you, Grandma used to say, *in her own crazy way.*

When we arrived at the hospital, Grandma was lying on the bed with her chin slightly tucked, like a sleeping baby. The bed seemed to envelop her. The room, too, was eerily silent. The staff had detached all the machines and wheeled them away.

"Oh, Grandma," I murmured. "You did it—you finally did it."

I couldn't see my mother through the film of my tears, but I could feel her move to the other side of the bed.

Grandma's cheek was cold and smooth as I kissed it, as were her hands, which someone had tucked under the sheet. Her belly was still warm.

As my mother took a seat, I caught something from out of the corner of my eye, like when I was on a foraging walk and encountered some unexpected flora or fungi. Hovering just below her navel, what the Chinese call the *Dan tian* or *Dan tien*—the main energy center of one's *chi*—I could make out the faint glimmering of something over my grandmother's body, like a swarm of illuminated miniature bees, or a celestial mass of glittery multihued lights. It was rather like what I'd envisioned fairy dust might look like when I was a child, the magical trail of Tinker Bell's wand. Though I couldn't entirely explain what I was seeing, I also wasn't surprised. Whatever I wasn't allowed to see in the ER, with Grandma focused and drawn to the beauty of something cosmic that I wasn't privy to, I was somehow, thankfully, being granted this.

I didn't say anything, but I was suddenly happy. This was the last of my grandmother, and she was almost, nearly, fully free.

My mother's cell phone rang—a ring tone that sounded like a European disco—and she jumped up from her seat. "We're here," she said, her voice booming through the room. "Come over when you can."

"Ma, shush," I said. "Lower your voice."

"That's your uncle," she said at the same volume, disregarding me. "He's on his way."

When Uncle Wesley arrived, he looked nervous and worried.

"Oh, Mommy, Mommy, Mommy," he said, shaking his hand inside his pocket so that the change rattled.

A nurse appeared at the curtain, clipboard in hand. "Excuse me," she said, addressing the three of us. "There are too many visitors here. Someone's going to have to leave."

My uncle and mom both looked up, their faces blank, infused with antidepressants. One of them—my mother, I think—began apologizing. My uncle looked like he was about to volunteer to go.

I was silently enraged. *Why were they being so accommodating? Why were we being so nice?* Suddenly, I hated our Asian politeness, our Chinese acquiescence to authority. I was sick of these nurses—doing their jobs but not listening, not seeing what was right in front of their eyes. I wanted to push the nurse out of the room.

I went to the curtain. "She's *dead*," I said, as pointedly as I could. "We're paying our respects."

The nurse looked over my shoulder and saw Grandma's body. Her face caved in, realizing her mistake. "I'm sorry—I didn't know," she said.

"It's all right," I said, closing the curtain as she backed away.

I was shaking when I turned to my family.

"Oh Mommy, Mommy, Mommy," my uncle said from his chair.

I returned my attention to my grandmother. Her belly was starting to feel a little cooler now, as if she'd been lingering in a drafty doorway.

A decade ago, my grandfather lay dying at this very hospital, and nearly thirty years before that, my mother, alone, pushed me out into the world. And here was Grandma, my brave little grandmother, having moved on to the beauty of something only the dying had the privilege to enter.

"You did it," I said, getting down near my grandmother's face. "I'm so proud of you—you were awesome to the very end."

My grandmother, my guru. The plant that mothered us all.

After we dispersed from the hospital, I found myself opening the door to my car, where a lifetime of Grandma-lessness yawned open before me.

It frightened me, this kind of blank numbness—worse than the whiteness of any page before I started writing, more terrifying than the first time I stood on a ski slope and encountered that gut-wrenching drop.

Instead of jumping into the car, I paused. Across the street was the park—a small wing of a larger park that I used to visit in college. I'd been passing it for decades on my way to my grandmother's house, but I'd never actually walked through it. Whenever we wanted a bit of greenery, we visited the Botanical Gardens.

It was hot and muggy, the kind of day where the air just seemed wet and heavy. I walked across the wide, heavily trafficked street, my T-shirt sticking to me, soaked under the armpits. Everything seemed dulled—the white figure of the "walk" signal before it became a blinking warning, the engine of the bus as it closed its doors and sped away, even the pain of my twisted ankle.

I arrived at the mouth of the park. In the distance, at the other edge of the park across a closed-off field, I could see teenagers shooting hoops and playing handball, the tops of blocky apartment buildings, a plane descending to nearby LaGuardia Airport. Behind me was the newest extension of the hospital—the oncology wing and the whirring noise of the rooftop air-conditioning units. I imagined that I could see through to the older building section, straight to my grandmother's room, nestled between the elevator banks, the corridors, and the nurses' stations.

I was standing under the shade of a small tree when I noticed that the ground was stained with deep purple splotches at my feet, as if someone had dropped several bottles of good Malbec on the ground. It smelled like I was standing inside a wine barrel. Above were branches heavily laden with fruit. Hundreds of clusters of reddish-purply-black berries.

I grabbed the nearest branch, knocking a few of the berries to the ground in my excitement. Growing around some leaves, in the middle of the branch, were several clusters of fruit just within reach. The ripest berry—a dark one hanging on a short stem that resembled a comma—dropped into my hand as soon as I touched it. Just as I'd read in Gibbons's *Stalking*, the berry was an aggregate fruit, resembling a cluster of deeply colored garnets, about the size of a cocoon.

Mulberries. All the signs were there. The right timing. The jewel-toned fruit. The alternate leaves that were serrated on the edges like teeth, and varied on every branch. One, shaped like a child's mitten, waved at me in the breeze.

Every act of foraging in the city, especially when I was about to take a bite of something I had only ever researched or read about, held a risk. But when coupled with my gut reaction that this was it—*this was what I'd been searching for all this time*—it became something more than that; it became an act of faith.

So I ate it.

The fruit was benignly sweet in my mouth, with none of the tartness of raspberries or blackberries. It was all smooth, mellow sweetness going down. I was so excited and relieved and thankful—*my grandmother had led me to the mulberries, she'd brought me to this very spot*—that I started grabbing more mulberries from that branch and all the other low-hanging ones around me.

I ate and ate until my belly was full and my mouth and hands were stained purple.

Mulberry-Balsamic Jam

My favorite way to eat mulberries, aside from straight from the branch, is as a jam or even in a vinaigrette. I like to cut the sweetness of the fruit with a good balsamic vinegar. Below is my jam recipe, which is made with Pomona's Universal Pectin and slightly less sugar than normally used. Wild mulberries are best, but one can also use store-bought blueberries or blackberries. Once opened, the jam should last about three weeks in the refrigerator.

>> **Yields 4 to 5 cups (Approximately 4 to 5 8 oz. [half pint] mason jars)**

4 cups stemmed mashed mulberries

¼ cup balsamic vinegar

2 teaspoons calcium water (made from a mixture of
   ½ teaspoon Pomona's calcium powder and ½ cup of
   water, shaken well)

2 teaspoons pectin powder

1 cup sugar

1. To sanitize, place the canning jars, rings, and lids into a giant pot filled with water; jars should be completely submerged. Bring to a roiling boil over high heat for at least 10 minutes; turn down the heat and allow the contents to stand in hot water.

2. In a separate pot, add the crushed mulberries, the balsamic vinegar, and the calcium water. Stir.

3. Mix the pectin powder into the sugar.

4. Bring the mulberry mixture to a boil. Add the pectin-sugar mixture and stir vigorously for 1 to 2 minutes to dissolve. Allow the mixture to return to a full boil, skimming off the foam that will accumulate on the edges. Remove the pot from heat.

5. Fill sterilized jars with jam to a quarter-inch of the top. Wipe rims clean before screwing on lids and rings. Place jars in giant water-filled pot, with enough water so that they are fully submerged. Boil for 10 minutes (add a minute for every 1,000 feet above sea level).

6. Remove the jars with tongs and allow them to cool on a countertop. Proper seals need to suck down (with some popping noises) to ensure that the jamming has been done correctly.

10

A Wild Lawn

Lambsquarters (*Chenopodium album*)

ater that afternoon, I found myself driving aimlessly
through my grandparents' old neighborhood, not wanting
to return to my mother's apartment, my sticky fingers loosely
maneuvering the steering wheel. I nosed the car past the cluster
of stores where we used to do our local shopping: the old pharmacy with the neon RX sign outside the door; the liquor store
owned by my grandfather's former boss and his wife, whom
my mother referred to as "the Dragon Lady"; the corner candy
shop where I went through my bubble gum and Tootsie Roll
and *Tiger Beat* magazine phases. I found myself passing all that,
and instead of turning off toward my mother's apartment, I was
crossing the big boulevard intersection toward my grandparents' old house.

To anyone else, our former home was just a plain, boxy-
looking mid-century two-story on a residential block near a

Lutheran church, tucked behind a gas station. But I've always loved it. It was the same house we lived in after I was born, the home of feasts and sleepovers until my grandparents moved to Flushing's Chinatown. The lawn to the side of the house belonging to the church was the soft, grassy area where I learned to walk, and where I played with my cousins whenever the neighborhood boys weren't hitting balls (disregarding the NO BALL PLAYING sign in the church window). There were tea roses along the perimeter near the church, and a secret side exit squeezed between it and our house that led to another lawn covered in grass and white clover. In the spring, yellow butter-cups blossomed until one day, mysteriously, they did not return.

If there was ever a house that I would haunt, it would be this one, I thought, parking the car and stepping out.

Nothing on the block looked like it had changed much in the time since we had moved, but the tea rose bush had long been dug up and what remained was just dirt and patches of grass. I was standing gingerly on my weak ankle, regarding the house, which looked shabbier and smaller than when we last lived there—everything always looked smaller now that I was older and no longer living in larger-than-life Los Angeles, where even the side streets were big and long and built with cars in mind. When I looked down, right next to my Ace-bandaged foot was a tall, stalky patch of lambsquarters.

It was rangy, with goosefoot-shaped leaves that dipped in the wind. I'd never much cared for it until my friend Deborah, who allowed lambsquarters to grow opportunistically in her garden in Ditmas Park, served it up blanched for me. That first bite of it cooked was a Popeye moment—lambsquarters had an outstanding green powerhouse punch. *I yam what I yam*, I thought, chomping down on another forkful. *And I like what I like.*

Standing on the old lawn, looking down at the *Chenopodium album*, was a homecoming of sorts—and suddenly I thought about my old stepfather, Jeffrey.

Jeffrey was the first man in our lives after my father left and the only one I'd ever called "Daddy." An amiable Jewish guy from the Bronx, he and my mother started dating when I was just a toddler; whenever he took my mom out, I wanted to go, too. Although I was worried at first that he'd steal her away from me, Jeffrey proved to be a patient and loving father—teaching me how to tie my shoes, and later attending my school performances. Tall and good-looking, he resembled Errol Flynn in *Robin Hood*, and I was convinced he'd steal from the rich to provide for us, even if he mostly walked around the apartment in slippers that permanently held the impression of his large toes.

Jeffrey was having job troubles, and when my mother discovered that he was hiding out in the neighborhood and then sneaking back into the apartment on the days he was supposedly looking for work, their relationship ended in a screaming match. I fell asleep that night with a pillow over my head to muffle the sounds of their arguing. The next day, when I returned home from school, Jeffrey was gone.

From that day forward, despite my grandparents' hopes that she would meet someone nice to take care of her—he didn't have to be Chinese, they'd given up on that idea after my father left—my mother swore she would never get married again. "I'm just not suited for it," she said.

But before they divorced, Jeffrey, who was a voracious reader and book-lover, told me something while sitting on the living room couch that had become his favorite place to read. "A great book is one you can continue to read and reread throughout your life," he said, using his finger as a bookmark inside a thick novel. "As you get older, you'll see things in it that you never noticed before."

I'd played on this patch of grass for years—had gotten its dirt in my mouth and stuck between my nails on numerous occasions throughout my childhood. And while I'd always noticed the delicate, showy flowers, and the bees and butterflies that congregated around them, I never knew that the very ground was edible. The lawn seemed to open like a book at my feet: Within a few yards of where I was standing, there were lambsquarters, and plantain rosettes, and lady's thumb with its dainty pink racemes, and heart-shaped violet leaves.

I gathered as much of the wild lambsquarters as I could, picking only the tops so the plants could continue to grow, stuffing a few leaves in my mouth along the way. I didn't know if it was because I'd just lost my grandmother or because of where they were growing, but the lambsquarters tasted somehow richer, denser, and more velvety than they'd ever tasted before.

Lambsquarters (*Chenopodium album*), alternately known as white goosefoot and pigweed, has wavy, diamond, or goosefoot-shaped leaves and a very distinctive mealy white or lavender powder in the center whorl of the new growth's tip that comes off in your fingertips. A member of the *Chenopodium* family, it is related to quinoa, beets, and spinach—making it a kind of superfood, high in vitamins A, C, and K, as well as riboflavin, niacin, calcium, manganese, and potassium.

Known as "fat-hen" in the United Kingdom, lambsquarters has been eaten as a food in Europe at least as far back as the Iron Age. The stomach of an excavated Iron Age man discovered in a bog in Grauballe, Denmark, contained the seeds of lambsquarters, as well as several other edible weeds and grasses. Native to the Mediterranean, *Chenopodium album* is a revered vegetable in Greek, Persian, and even Bangladeshi cuisine, but despite its long-held uses, can be difficult to find at a farmers' market.

The best places to find wild lambsquarters are in meadows or fields, as they prefer full sunlight. (*Note:* Lambsquarters can pick up heavy metals from the ground, so if you're collecting from the same spot over a lengthy period of time you may want to get the soil tested. See Appendix.)

The next morning, I removed the lambsquarters and four eggs from the refrigerator. I dunked the *Chenopodium album* stalks in a bowl of water before cracking the eggs open and scrambling them with a fork. As I fished the lambsquarters out, shaking them to release any dirt that might be clinging to the leaves, a black bug the size of an ink dot swam out, its legs furiously working through the water.

"Sorry, little tyke," I said, pouring the water and the bug down the kitchen drain.

Like spinach, lambsquarters cooks up quickly, turning a deep forest green in a matter of minutes. Soon, I was setting down a plateful of scrambled eggs Florentine—what I called Scrambled Eggs "Lambsquarterine"—in front of my mother in the living room.

Even though she had never heard of lambsquarters, Mom was still my grandfather's daughter and gamely dug in with her fork.

"That's good," my mother said, swallowing.

I watched with pride as she ate another forkful. I looked at her the same way my grandfather had regarded me whenever I gobbled up one of his meals.

The lambsquarters gave the dish a verdant flavor that was more deeply penetrating than even organic farmers' market spinach. I could practically taste the healthy vitamins working their way down my esophagus to my chest and out toward my fingertips after I took my first bite. *Home-style, homegrown lambsquarters.*

It felt so completely satisfying to make a meal from foraged ingredients off the soil of our old home and share it with my mother. I hadn't felt that comforted since before my grandmother's decline.

"Now that Grandma's gone," I said, sitting on the floor and crossing my legs crossed the way I used to as a teenager, "*you* have to be the one to meet my boyfriends."

I envisioned introducing my future beaus to my mom, who instead of ignoring them and turning the conversation onto herself would ask them questions, trying to ascertain their character and motivations just like Grandma had done.

"Why?" Mom said, finishing the last of her eggs. "I'll just meet the guy when you decide to get married."

"Ma, you can't—it doesn't work that way."

"Why not?" she said, smiling girlishly and looking at me with an expression as if to say, *Why do I have to do anything differently?*

Scrambled Eggs "Lambsquarterine"

My favorite way to serve lambsquarters is in a savory pie, but if I have no time for baking, it also makes a delicious breakfast.

>> **Yields 2 servings**

4 large organic eggs
1 teaspoon extra virgin olive oil
2 cups lambsquarters, washed and roughy chopped
salt and pepper to taste

1. In a bowl, crack the eggs and scramble with a fork. Set aside.

2. Heat the oil over medium-low heat in a frying pan. Add the lambsquarters, and sauté until the lambsquarters turns a deep forest green, about a minute or less.

3. Add the eggs to the pan, stirring into the lambsquarters. Heat only a few minutes until the eggs appear still wet; cut flame.

4. Add the salt and pepper and stir mixture in pan; when done, eggs should still have a creamy, custard-like consistency.

11

A Recipe for Forgiveness

Blackberry (*Rubus allegheniensis*)

I t's another brutally hot July morning as I climb over the park's stone wall, landing feetfirst in the wood chips under the oak trees where every fall the squirrels forage for acorns. Even though it is hours before noon, I am already perspiring. I straighten my knapsack on my shoulders and trudge through the wood mulch, bouncy under my sandals. It is the first time I am taking a walk back in Brooklyn without the support of a bandage on my ankle, and it feels good.

The picnic area is filled with stroller moms, kids on bikes with training wheels, and families setting up barbeques, the sharp smell of lighter fluid hanging in the air. I can hear the crisp sound of a carbonated drink being opened, children screaming, the splash of their feet under sprinklers. In the distance, a counselor's whistle as summer campers sporting yellow T-shirts race toward a soccer ball being kicked across the field.

In the weeks since Grandma died, I discovered a giant, sprawling red mulberry tree here, and even though it's the end of the season, I'm hoping to collect the last bit of tenacious fruit that might still be lingering. Even if I can't collect enough for a pie or a jam, whatever fruit is left on the tree, even a few berries, will be enough to satisfy me.

I received generous comments on my Fort Greene mulberry story—some lovely condolences and reminiscences of childhood mulberry picking from readers throughout the city. Nearly every commenter knew of a tree growing around the neighborhood, from Fort Greene Park to a prodigious fruiter on nearby Adelphi Street. One longtime resident, a gardener in a former community lot, was familiar with the tree we profiled.

"The mulberry is a volunteer—probably from a seed dropped by a bird that maybe ate a berry from the Adelphi tree," wrote George W. "A fitting reminder to Ava that new generations thrive from the seeds of foremothers (and fathers)."

The weeks after Grandma's death had been particularly challenging.

While family flew in from California and Maryland, I juggled writing Grandma's eulogy with taking care of my mother, who underwent foot surgery and couldn't walk without the aid of crutches. I was back in my mother's apartment again, being yelled at for doing everything the wrong way, all the while running around on my own aching ankle, relying heavily on a bag of dried motherwort to get me through—chewing bits of leaves that became soggy in my mouth.

At the times in which I felt like I couldn't do anything to please my mother, I ate some motherwort. When I awoke in the mornings crying from the loss of my grandmother, I ate motherwort. I put my dating life on hold indefinitely, or at least until I was finished grieving, and I nibbled on some more. The herb was so calming that I continued eating it until the motherwort disappeared from the bag, and all that was left at the bottom were stray dry bits that resembled crushed oregano.

I attended a meditation retreat with about six hundred others in Easton, Massachusetts, led by Thich Nhat Hanh. I was new to the teachings of the Vietnamese Zen master, but a friend had loaned me a CD of his dharma talks some months back, and I'd loved hearing about his work with French children. ("Breathing in, *Oui, oui, oui.* Breathing out, *Merci, merci, merci.*") The multilingualism worked—I listened to the CD in my car, and anytime some crazy driver cut me off, instead of cursing him, I'd silently breathe French *yeses* and *thank-yous* in and out.

Over the course of the five-day retreat, Thich Nhat Hanh and his dharma talk leaders used metaphors and language based in the natural world that struck home to me. His energetic second-in-command, Sister Chan, led us in a soothing practice called "Touching the Earth," in which we collectively poured our old sorrows and grievances into the ground to be reborn into "flowers of understanding." (By the end of it, I was one of several people sobbing throughout the hall.) In one of his evening dharma talks, Thich Nhat Hanh instructed us to consider our parents as fresh, young plants long before they had us, when they were just kids themselves.

I thought of my handsome wayward father as a teenager, attending Stuyvesant High School and playing basketball on the streets of Chinatown, the oldest son who could do no wrong in his father's eyes.

I thought of my mother, the little beauty, growing up in Queens, with a facility for other languages—including French and German—long before she met my father and was crowned Miss Chinatown.

"If you study a plant when it sprouts from seed, and then again when it is fully grown," Thich Nhat Hahn said, sitting in lotus position on the stage, "is it the same or different?"

Seeing my parents as both images—how they once were compared to how they appeared now—gave me a new sense of openness. It was like standing on the wide-open prairie in Boulder, Colorado, surrounded by sun-synthesizing motherwort, finding myself with new foraging eyes and able to breathe again.

They were the same, yet different. And so was I.

Instead of going back home from the retreat, I stopped off first in Queens. It was time to put down the old hurt and anger, and allow it all to blossom into a Buddhist *flower of understanding*. I picked up dinner for both my mother and me along the way.

"Mom, I'm sorry," I said over the sound of the blaring television. We were sitting in her living room eating eggplant Parmesan. "I'm sorry I was so mad at you for so many years."

My mother's round face reflected a jumble of emotions from where she sat on the sofa, until it settled into a slight frown. "I know, you have high expectations of people," she said.

Then she brought up the letter I'd written her when I was nineteen—the good-bye letter listing all of my childhood grievances. The parade of boyfriends and my feeling abandoned. The threats to send me to live with my father.

"When you have a daughter," she said, mustering up all the outer-boroughs attitude that she could, "I'm going to give it to you and throw it back in your face."

I flinched, as if she had physically hit me. But if she noticed, she didn't react.

"It's okay, Ma," I said, swallowing the bitterness of my own disappointment, and any expectations that I'd had of us making up. "It's an apology—you don't have to do anything except acknowledge it."

Showing vulnerability was difficult for my mother, and acknowledging my saying I was sorry meant that she had to admit to being hurt—something she'd never done before any man, friend, or family member, even me.

She shrugged, returning to her television program. "Oh, okay," she said.

I am walking across patches of balding grass, toward the sprawling red *Morus* tree still several yards away, hoping that I can find those mulberries that remind me so much of my grandmother. Even though they'll never be a substitute for losing her, in light of the other night's disappointing conversation with my mother, perhaps the fruit will offer some sort of solace.

As I near the mulberry tree, the ground is littered with the crushed remnants of mulberries, over which the flies are dizzily buzzing. As I get closer, I am met with that smell of fermenting wine again—as if I'm standing inside a giant wine cask. Euell Gibbons recalled the joys of climbing mulberry trees as a child in *Stalking the Wild Asparagus*—he was so good at doing it while barefoot that he earned the nickname "Toes." ("My own childhood would have been infinitely poorer without this most familiar of all wild fruits," he wrote.) While I'd love to kick off my own shoes, I would look too conspicuous scaling this *Morus* tree in such a well-populated area of the park. Instead,

I'll settle for grabbing whatever fruit I can within my limited arms' reach.

Even though the mulberry tree is quite tall—stories taller than the one I found in Flushing—it has several low-lying branches, so even I can grasp them. I am salivating, thinking of gorging myself on the berries' sweetness, but when I grab the nearest branch, all I can see are clusters of leaves growing in alternating patterns with no berries in sight.

I grab the next branch. And then another. All of them are empty. I shake the branches in desperation, hoping some hidden mulberries will drop. I shake and shake until my arm feels numb, and I start to feel parental eyes watching me from a distance. But nothing falls except for the occasional mitten-shaped leaf.

I look with dismay at all of the rotting mulberries at my feet.

I want to cry. I've missed it. I've missed the timing of the mulberries, and all I'm left with are drunken flies circling my ankles.

I continue my walk toward the meadow, which is filled with the kind of wet midsummer haze reminiscent of my childhood. The clover, plantain, and grasses are matted in patches where the echoes of weekend softball games still linger.

I'm still sad, and angry at myself for not coming out sooner, as I enter the wooded area where the wood sorrel and the garlic mustard grow. It's cooler here but just as humid, the smell of moist earth in the air as I lean forward and make my way up the rise. A mosquito buzzes by my ear.

By the old oak, the ground is covered in a carpet of false Solomon's seal and enchanter's nightshade, the tiny burrs catching on the bottoms of my pants. A long log carries the remnants of a whitish fungus, resembling a decaying version of the fan-shaped oyster mushrooms I've seen on the plates of high-end restaurants. When I bend down to inspect it, it's a wet, mushy, pulpy mess under my fingertips. Once again, I've arrived too late in a plant or a mushroom's cycle. At the slightest touch, chunks of mushroom break off and fall to the ground. My fingers smell like funky, decaying wood—a strangely intoxicating scent, and for a moment I can't stop sniffing them.

Years ago, my mother admitted that even before her wedding day to my stepfather, she knew that getting married to him was a mistake. Later she told me that she was acting in the shadow of something my father had said to her in an angry fit many years ago.

"Who's going to want you—a single mother with a baby? You'll never find anyone to love you."

It was such a mean thing to say to a twenty-four-year-old pregnant woman that all I can conclude was that he was trying to manipulate her into not having me, the last-ditch efforts of a desperate man.

Luckily, my mother had the fortitude to give birth to me anyway, but those words stuck in her head. So six years later she married my stepfather, even though she knew that it was a mistake.

Perhaps if they'd met before she and Stanley had gotten engaged, before the accidental pregnancy, without the pressure of having to find a partner and new father for me, things might have been different. Perhaps like today's foraging walk, the timing was simply off. Or perhaps, instead of believing my father, she simply should have trusted herself.

As I walk the hills and rises toward the highest point in the park, I pass the log where the reishi mushrooms grow and count three new reddish semicircles of growth; stands of poor man's pepper (*Lepidium virginicum*), which resemble pipe cleaners and have a wasabi-like kick; and a cluster of Asiatic dayflower

(*Commelina communis*) with an edible blossom so transient that it could be a Buddhist lesson in impermanence.

I climb the stone stairs where the urban boot-campers race one another, sweating profusely with each step, and turn a corner where the mugwort grows high and edges out the other plants, even the lambsquarters. *Artemisia vulgaris* was widely used in medicine, charms, and spells in parts of Western Europe, and used to flavor beer in England before the discovery of hops. In Asia, it's burned as medicine to turn breech babies and get rid of "cold" spots in the body. I have friends who've drunk mugwort tea to intensify their dreams, but I don't need it to do what my brain does naturally.

I've stopped several yards away from the top to collect plantain leaves to take the sting out of my mosquito-bitten arms. I'm smearing crushed plantain against my skin, leaving cooling green streaks, when I notice a small black thing about the size of a dime drop from a tangle of bushes and roll straight onto the path. Peering into the bushes, I see dozens of blackberries under a canopy of arching stems with palmate, compound-shaped leaves. I quickly make a grab and nearly fall headlong into them, thorny tendrils catching on my shirt and knapsack.

Unlike benign mulberry trees, which give up their fruit easily, blackberries come swaddled in thorns. *Edible Wild Plants* and the Peterson Field Guides describe them as growing off long canes that spread like thickets. I soon learn firsthand that getting hold of these juicy berries is an object lesson in patience, as I navigate the obstacle course of hooked reddish thorns.

Through the help of experts at the Brooklyn Botanic Gardens, I later discover that these blackberries are *Rubus alleghenniensis*, or "Allegheny blackberry." Allegheny blackberries have alternate oval-shaped leaves with three to seven leaflets that are a paler green underneath, and can be found in fields, abandoned lots, and parkland across the eastern United States as well as parts of the Midwest and California. As with mulberries, the fruit form an aggregate cluster, making for a juicy taste experience in the height of summer. (In England, the berries are as large as quarters, but our native Allegheny blackberries are smaller and tarter.)

I'm on my hands and knees deep in the heart of the blackberry patch, and every time I move another thorn tugs at my skin and clothing. I'm looking for the ripest berry I can find among the dangling fruit, when I spot it—the blackest blackberry I've ever seen, hanging from a spiny stem surrounded by immature red fruit.

Instead of making a mad dash for it, I slowly, methodically navigate around the tangle of thorny canes, avoiding catching any on my sleeve where they will eventually spring back to hit me in the face. A starling-like bird lands in the canopy several paces from me, regarding me warily before grabbing a berry and flying away.

My fingers are now around the cool, jewel-like fruit.

It is a tart and zingy surprise in my mouth—much tarter and citrusy than any store-bought blackberry. It takes all my willpower not to pop every berry I can find straight into my mouth.

I spend the next twenty minutes collecting them—purplyblack blackberries, ones that are the color of jet, berries that are still partially reddish—crouching down on my newly healed ankle, my hands stained like a wine cork, not even bothered by the prickly thorns.

For years, the fact that my father walked out when my mother was pregnant with me defined me.

It was a terrible truth. As a sentence, it implied a causal relationship that I translated into *My father left because of me.* And as a kid, I figured that the following must also be true: Because he left, *I* was the one who ruined my mother.

All that time growing up in Flushing, my mother and I acted as if our resources were scarce—there was never enough time or love or money to go around to sustain us.

But, in truth, there was plenty all around. We just didn't know where to look.

Blackberry-Buckwheat Pancakes

I've adapted this from a Molly Wizenberg recipe, where she uses the marvelous *Cook's Illustrated* technique of mixing melted butter with egg yolk first, allowing the butter to better incorporate into the rest of the batter and thereby creating these yummy-licious pancakes.

Wild American Allegheny blackberries are much smaller than cultivated blackberries, or the species I've seen growing wild in England; you can add several blackberries to these pancakes depending on their size. I prefer small pancakes the size of dollops and so add only one or two berries to the middle of each. Like Wizenberg suggests, allow the pancakes to cook on one side first, and then flip when ready (about a minute), before adding any fruit.

>> **Yields at least 8 medium pancakes, and more than 10 "silver-dollar" pancakes**

²/₃ cup unbleached all-purpose flour

¹/₃ cup buckwheat flour

1 teaspoon sugar

$^1/_4$ teaspoon salt

$^1/_2$ teaspoon baking powder

$^1/_4$ teaspoon baking soda

$^3/_4$ cup buttermilk

$^1/_4$ cup plus 2 tablespoons milk

1 large egg, separated

2 tablespoons unsalted butter, melted

2 tablespoons canola oil, for pan

$^1/_2$ pint or 6 oz. blackberries

1. In a bowl whisk together your dry ingredients: both flours, sugar, salt, baking powder, and baking soda.

2. In a separate bowl add the buttermilk and milk; whisk in the egg white.

3. In a smaller bowl, mix the egg yolk and the melted butter; stir into milk mixture.

4. Add the wet mixture to the dry ingredients and whisk; be careful not to overmix.

5. Heat a skillet over medium-high heat and add 1 table-spoon of canola oil to coat the pan. To test if the pan is hot enough, add a small droplet of batter; if it starts to sizzle and cook, it's ready.

6. Add the batter in quantities depending upon your pan-cake-size preference; I like small "silver dollar" pancakes, so I use a favorite soupspoon. Don't overcrowd the pan. Flip the pancakes when they start to bubble and set around the edges, 2 to 3 minutes.

7. Add the blackberries; if you are doing the "silver-dollar" method, use only 1 or 2. Cook until the pancakes are browned underneath, about 2 minutes. Remove from pan and keep warm.

8. Re-oil the pan and continue.

12

A Mysterious Fungus

(*Chlorophyllum molybdites*)

One particularly humid morning, I was walking along a park road, returning home from a foraging walk. It had rained the night before and the ground was still moist under my feet. Everything in the park seemed vibrant and alive—cyclists in multicolored spandex whizzing by on expensive bikes, joggers running past with earplugs dangling, older Korean women in long-sleeved shirts sporting giant sun visors. I was noting the red clover blossoms, grown to giant proportions, lining the bridle path, when I approached a grassy triangular meridian.

From the corner of my eye, I saw the flash of something white. Sometimes it's nothing but a piece of paper or a candy wrapper, but this time I discovered a perfectly globe-shaped mushroom as large as a lollipop. It was lightly covered in brown scales, and hefty like a small microphone in my hand. I sniffed the tightly closed cap, inhaling the deliciously earthy scent. My heart started pounding so loudly I could hear it in my ears. I had no idea what kind of mushroom this was, but I was trying to learn from past mistakes: Last fall, I'd discovered a crop of scaly, torpedo-shaped mushrooms on the lawn outside my office, which, being unfamiliar fungi, I hesitated to even touch. I later learned from the Missouri Department of Conservation's website, which had beautiful illustrations of a sampling of edible fungi, that they were highly delectable shaggy manes. Although I kept an eye out for them for months, I never saw them again; even today, I cursed myself for being such a scaredy-cat that I didn't even bring a sample home to identify.

Not this time, I thought, searching for a paper bag in my knapsack to put it in.

It was then that I spied another mushroom only a few feet away, and then another even larger one right next to it. In fact, I was standing inside a classic fairy ring of mushrooms.

I was greedy and gathered all of them—about a dozen in total—keeping my head down and trying not too draw too much attention to myself.

Back home, I knew exactly whom to call.

William Parsons was a senior member and former president of the New York Mycological Society, a venerable mushroom club established in the late 1800s. American composer John Cage—who was so wild about fungi that he created entire musical scores based on mushroom sites—was a co-founder who had revived and revamped the club, turning it into a *Society* in the

1960s. *The New York Times Local* had dubbed Bill the "Mushroom Man," and I had seen a video of him seated at his piano, affably singing the society's anthem.

I described my mushrooms to him over the phone, including the fairy ring and where I'd found them.

"Did you do a spore print?" Bill asked.

I didn't have a clue about what that was, so Bill invited me over to show me how to make one.

I hung up the phone. My initiation into real mushroom identification was about to begin.

I arrived at Bill's brownstone the next day with my mushroom booty in two large paper bags. I followed him into his open kitchen, where we inspected my samples on a wooden cutting board. The first thing to check for, he informed me, was whether or not the mushroom had gills or pores. My specimens were so young that they were like closed, rounded umbrellas, so Bill cut into the bottom of one with a paring knife, discarding the stem.

"They're gilled," he said, revealing the feather-fine white ridges running underneath the cap.

He flipped through the pages of a hardcover book, *Mushrooms of North America* by Orson Miller, before stopping at a page filled with pictures of mushrooms that resembled my specimens.

"See these brown scales?" Bill pointed to the dark, peeling spots on the pictured cap. "They're characteristic of shaggy parasols, which are edible."

Shaggy parasols. They had a similar name to the *shaggy manes* I'd passed up on campus.

Bill flipped a page in his book. "Or they could be the green-spored *Lepiota*—the false parasol," he said. "*Chlorophyllum molybdites*, which are poisonous."

My stomach sank. "Oh," I said.

"We won't know for sure until we make a spore print." Bill rummaged around his desk for some paper.

"Ideally, you'll want to use colored paper," he said, waving a pad in front of me with slightly shaky hands.

If the mushroom were a shaggy parasol it would have white spores, he explained, but if it were the other unpronounceable one, a green print would appear.

He scraped away the remaining ring of flesh at the bottom of the mushroom, and laid it gill-side down on the paper. Then, he placed a glass jar over it.

"Check in with me tomorrow," he said. "It'll be ready by then."

I thanked him and left him a gift of half of the mushrooms.

A mushroom is the fruiting body of an underground network of mycelium, and when it comes to foraging, it's the idea of eating wild ones that makes most people nervous. Periodically, when I tell someone I've just met about my gathering practices, that person will invariably bring up a popular myth surrounding Euell Gibbons. "Didn't he die from eating a poisonous mushroom?" (This is untrue: Gibbons died from complications with Marfan syndrome, a genetic disorder of the connective tissues.) But since I had no desire to have my stomach pumped for eating something potentially poisonous, I decided to make my own spore print, too.

Later that evening, I cleared a place on my writing desk, and assembled two pieces of paper—one cantaloupe-colored, the other white—and a glass florist's vase. I cut off the mushroom stem and scraped off the thin layer on the bottom of the cap (the "veil"); then, I placed the mushroom down on both papers and the vase, upside down, covering it.

The mushroom cap resembled a marshmallow that had been toasted on the top. I sat there and watched it perspire under the glass, thinking of all the wonderful meals I could have. Linguini with sautéed mushrooms. Mushroom bruschetta. Thinly sliced mushrooms on pizza with olive oil drizzled on top.

I became so hungry that I found it difficult to fall asleep.

For nearly a month after Grandma died, I woke up in the mornings filled with the overwhelming compulsion to forgive.

I thought about my father and his disappearances, and then I forgave him.

Because I could not force my mother to forgive Stanley for walking out, I did the next best thing—I acknowledged her pain, and then I forgave her for not forgiving him.

And then because my grandparents were no longer around, I forgave them, too, for not forgiving him.

Finally, I forgave all of us for not getting over it, for carrying the pain and anger with us for so many years.

The hardest thing, I found, was forgiving myself.

Even if I can't forgive myself now, I will in the near future, I thought, making the vow to the dappled ceiling above me.

I imagined a string of underground mycelium threads as large and wide as the city itself, breaking down the old root structures of unnecessary things, with a mighty force capable of busting through earth and asphalt, and wondered what new creations would suddenly arise from it.

I woke up the next morning to find condensation lining the inside of the vase and my mushroom shrunken like an old potato. Underneath the cap, a faint, greenish-beige spore print remained on the paper. It was shaped like a starburst with a hole in the center.

My heart sank. I had in the refrigerator a half dozen green-spored *Lepiota*. *Chlorophyllum molybdites*. The *false* parasol.

Because of its close resemblance to the edible shaggy parasol (*Chlorophyllum rhacodes*), *Chlorophyllum molybdites* was one of the leading causes of mushroom poisonings in North America, according to mycology professor Tom Volk. Symptoms include vomiting, severe diarrhea, upset stomach, nausea, bleeding from the gut, and blue lips, tongue, and fingernails.

"You probably won't die from eating this mushroom (although there is one recorded fatality involving a child), but it's certainly not a pleasant dining experience," wrote Volk on his Fungi-of-the-month site. "So be very careful if you plan on eating any *Lepiota* species. Projectile diarrhea would not be very much fun."

I immediately called Bill. His spore print had appeared green as well.

I felt really bad about leaving him a gift of all those poisonous mushrooms. Even though others before me had been fooled by the green-spored *Lepiota*, I still felt rather duped— like a tourist who bought a fake designer purse for a "steal" from a guy on a street corner. Luckily, Bill had seen his fair share of gut-wrenching fungi in his time, and one more batch by a rank amateur wasn't going to kill him. I hung up and tossed my bag of remaining mushrooms into the trash.

Thank God we'd made our spore prints! I didn't want to think about how many days of being curled up into a ball on the bathroom floor I would have had to endure if I'd eaten the entire batch.

How to Make a Mushroom Spore Print

In the dizzying range of wild mushrooms that can grow around us, one of the best tools for identifying an unknown specimen is to make a spore print. Spore prints, which come in a host of different colors and shapes depending on the mushroom, are a necessity for proper identification, along with consulting experts and reputable guidebooks. For fun, you can also consider joining your local mycological society.

1. *Determining your paper color.* Refer to a good mushroom reference guide, such as Lincoff's *National Audubon Society Field Guide to North American Mushrooms* or Michael Kuo's Mushroom Expert website, and look up the mushroom yours most resembles; then, note the color of the spores. This will help you determine if it's best to use white or colored paper for your print. For example, if your mushroom has white spores, you can use a sheet of colored paper or even a sheet of glass. If it has dark chocolate spores, then of course plain white paper is fine.

2. If your mushroom is in a young button form, cut off the bottom, along with the stem, to free the spores.

3. Place the mushroom gill-side or pore-side down on a sheet of paper. When in doubt, you can hedge your bets by using white and colored paper laid side by side next to each other, laying your mushroom across both.

4. Cover with a glass vase or jar overnight, or at least for several hours.

5. The following morning, uncover the jar and gently lift the mushroom. A beautiful spore print will be revealed.

SPRING

13

The Yellow Morel

Morel mushrooms (*Morchella esculenta*)

Every April, the New York Mycological Society (NYMS) opened the mushroom hunting season with a morel breakfast and hunt exclusively for members just north of the city. It had been an unusually warm and early spring, with many of the flowering trees bursting forth weeks ahead of schedule, and many of us were uncertain how that would affect today's hunt. I'd been inspired to join the club and its enthusiastic band of mycologists a few weeks after meeting Bill Parsons, and now here I was standing on a backyard deck, with Owen and about sixty other members, itching to go mushroom hunting after the winter hiatus. As we chomped down on bagels and pastries, the anticipation for morels, some of the choicest edible mushrooms available in the wild, was palpable.

I'd met Owen six months before at a party in my neighborhood. Tall and British, with an easy smile and an affectionate spontaneity that I soon discovered when he wrapped me in a bear hug within the first few hours of knowing each other, Owen felt instantly familiar. He walked me home through the tree-lined streets that night, and from that point forward throughout the fall and winter, he became my new foraging partner—helping me to gather autumn acorns and gingko nuts to transform into hearty breads and appealing appetizers; tapping a maple tree in Fort Greene in the middle of January to create a sublime maple syrup; even traveling from Manhattan's Upper East Side, where he lived, out to Brooklyn just to dig my car out of the snow. Although Owen was separated from a wife in Germany, and we hadn't been dating for very long, this was our second official mushroom hunt as a couple. We even had a joint NYMS "family" membership together.

Ahead of us, a seasoned mushroom forager, carrying a string of dried porcini in one hand and gesticulating with the other, was conversing with Paul Sadowski about a specific type of *Morchella* they would both be looking for.

Paul, whom I'd gotten to know through the various club walks and identification sessions, looked at her with expressive eyes above the red-knotted handkerchief around his neck. Aside from being the club secretary, he'd also worked closely with John Cage, who had decades ago introduced him to the joys of mycology.

"I'll be *you know where*," Paul said, smiling. I could have sworn that he winked.

Because these mushrooms were so coveted (upward of $70 a pound, fresh) and had a tendency to come up in the same place every year, many morel hunters were secretive about their special spots.

Some newer members were studying a handful of morel samples—grooved and honeycombed, and shaped rather like comical, leaning hats—laid out in a basket. There were tan-colored *Morchella esculenta* (meaning "succulent and delicious" in Latin) with their deep, rich flavor and earthy aromatics that were so delightful in French cuisine; smaller, pointier *Morchella deliciosa*; a black morel (*Morchella elata*); and semi-libre or *Morchella semilibera*, which because of their rather phallic shape had earned the nickname "peckerheads."

Today, we would be scouring the forest floor for the yellow *Morchella esculenta*. Morels were notoriously difficult to spot, so after the food was devoured, Paul held up the basket of *Morchella* for all the newbies like us to study in the hopes that it would help with pattern recognition. Then, we packed up and headed out toward the secret location—an abandoned and overgrown apple orchard near a running stream where patches of watercress thrived.

Fellow member Jason Cortlund gave us the tip to look for morels under trees with which they had symbiotic relationships, i.e., "elm, tulip, and apple trees." *Morchella*'s only lookalike was the "false morel," which unlike a real one was thick all the way through (true morels were hollow) and rather resembled a morel having a meltdown.

Club vice president Dennis Aita was yards ahead of us, leading the pack. Aside from being the club's *Agaricus* expert, Dennis had the distinction of having once found a dead body hanging in the woods while foraging for mushrooms with another member (one of my biggest fears). At the time, they were so keen on taking advantage of the good mushroom weather that they actually debated when to call the authorities (the man had been dead, apparently, for some time). To their credit, they called right away.

I didn't actually see Dennis give the signal, but suddenly everyone around us took off, fanning out with baskets and paper bags. It was the closest I had ever been to the frenzy of a truffle hunt, and the energy was frenetic. Owen and I could have trailed one of the senior members, but I liked the surprise of finding something entirely on my own, and so we headed out to a less visibly crowded section of the woods.

After hiking through some pretty thick bramble, we came upon a swampy area where the skunkweed grew as large as cabbages and the sunlight washed out the surrounding trees so brightly that they appeared white and thin and ghostly. I scoured the landscape for ramps—young springtime oniony shoots that over the past few years were appearing on the plates of fancy restaurants throughout town. Owen knelt down among the moss and lichen with his camera and snapped pictures.

The weekend before I had turned forty, and Owen and Heidi had thrown me a big birthday bash at her communal brown-stone in Fort Greene. I'd been apprehensive about my birth-day before meeting Owen, but somehow just knowing that we were together, surrounded by old friends and colleagues, and celebrating in a place whose very ground and vegetation I was intimate with, made everything seem all right.

Owen gave a toast in front of the entire gathering. "If you're lucky enough like I am to know Ava, you might find yourself in the unlikeliest of places—either on a mushroom hunt, or root-ing around for acorns. I love her very much," Owen said, raising his glass. "I wish that I had met her twenty years earlier—it would have saved me a lot of trouble."

There was a collective murmur of *ahhs* throughout the room, and even days later, I could still feel the warmth of his words.

I had just scaled the remnants of an old, low-lying stone wall, when I spied several yards away a brownish-white shelf mushroom on the bottom of a tree so old and worn that it resembled my apartment's floor planks. I crept down under a thick canopy of crisscrossing thickets, the wild garlic brushing against my jeans, and discovered four perfectly formed dryad's saddles as large as my fist. Also known as pheasant's back mushrooms, these brown-scaled polypores resembled the speckled plumage of a female pheasant. I'd first seen *Polyporus squamosus* on a tour with the Wildman, where we encountered one the size of a dinner plate. Dryad's saddles were a far cry from delectable morels, but I added them to my basket anyway.

Owen and I continued walking, searching for *Morchella* under the new spring shoots and last year's foliage. We uncovered springy strands of wild garlic, rounded garlic mustard in its first-year form, and toothed dandelion leaves, but no morels.

We found a partially shaded spot where the ground was soft and level, where we ate our lunch while the wind gently shook a twisted apple tree above us. Although I checked, the terrain was sadly free of morels.

"Everything came up so early this year," I said, watching a few NYMS members walk by in the distance with baskets in hand. "I'm not sure the morels are even around anymore."

After a few more hours of fruitlessly navigating through thorny bramble, we reassembled with the rest of the morel hunters near the orchard's entrance. Our basket was empty except for those dryad's saddles I'd collected.

"End of the season," someone murmured behind me. "Slim pickings."

I was staring out across the road, disappointed, when I looked down and noticed a short patch of stalky weeds only a few feet away. I crouched and noted the hairy stems and opposite-growing deeply green leaves. It was same plant that Brigitte Mars had growing around her Boulder, Colorado, home. *Stinging nettles.*

"Every schoolkid in England knows to avoid that plant,"

Owen said, frowning, as I pulled plastic bags from my pockets. "What are you doing?"

"Gathering tea." I wrapped my hands inside the bags, transforming them into makeshift gloves, and began plucking some of the plant's new growth from the top.

Despite growing up in a country practically covered in nettles, Owen had never consumed them.

One of the stingers wormed its way through the bag and pierced my finger. "Ouch!" I said.

Owen looked at my red, throbbing fingertip. "I'll find some burdock—it helps take the sting out."

"You know burdock?" Most people I knew had never heard of the plant, unless they were herbalists or foodie types.

I watched, strangely pleased, as Owen poked his nose along the edges of the road. He returned a few minutes later with a broad, fuzzy leaf. When he crushed the burdock against my finger, it was instant relief.

"How'd you know to do that?" I asked.

"It's something I was taught as a child," he said. "How did you know that you could prepare nettle tea?"

"It's something I made it my business to learn," I replied, smiling.

I was trying not to show it, but I was a little worried about the "Urban Forager." The previous month, Andy had brought me over to the City Room—the high-profile online section of *The New York Times* that focused on the five boroughs—where he'd recently been promoted to editor. Wanting to make a big splash, I wrote about the daylilies that grew wild around the Central Park reservoir and Staten Island's Greenbelt.

I had been introduced to the Central Park daylily patch by

Steve Brill the year before. One bite of the fresh shoot and I was hooked—they tasted like string beans sautéed in garlic and sesame oil. While I'd discovered hidden patches in Prospect Park, by far the largest one was in Central Park, where the day-lilies grew in a wild jumble, by the hundreds if not thousands, willy-nilly along a hillside near the reservoir.

After the story was posted, the comments came stream-ing in—some interested, some fearful, nearly everyone excited and weighing in on the pleasures and horrors of city foraging. Some opposed the very idea because they were dubious about the quality of the soil; others questioned the legalities of forag-ing in the park.

But then, someone with the handle *A. Benepe* posted a com-ment on the site about a proposal to allow a supermarket to harvest plants in Prospect Park, and introduced the concept of foraging licenses. Our readers were up in arms, and not just because the Parks commissioner was named Adrian Benepe; some demanded that the *Times* investigate.

Andy contacted the commissioner. The comment turned out to be a hoax—Benepe denied having posted it—but the message was clear. It was illegal to take anything from the park.

The commissioner pointed us to Section 1-04 under "Pro-hibited Uses": "No person shall deface, write upon, sever, muti-late, kill or remove from the ground any plants, flowers, shrubs or other vegetation under the jurisdiction of the Department without permission of the Commissioner." (This fell under the same section that prohibited chasing pigeons, using metal detectors, walking along newly seeded grass, spitting on a mon-ument, or failing to pick up after one's dog.)

"If fifteen people decide to go harvest daylilies to stir-fry that night," Benepe said, "you could wipe out the entire popula-tion of daylilies around the Central Park reservoir."

Because Steve Brill and others had regularly led foraging walks within the public parks for years, I'd always considered foraging a kind of nebulous gray area. Sure, park rangers didn't want you digging up trees or planted ornamentals, but they wouldn't stop you from collecting ginkgoes or dandelions. Plus, the Parks Department *had* hired Brill to lead tours there after he'd been arrested for eating weeds. Especially since most of the plants that I wrote about were considered *weeds*, and were unwanted, alien invasives that Parks Department workers regularly attempted to eradicate with pesticides, including garlic mustard, Japanese knotweed, and Asiatic dayflower, I considered what we foragers did a more efficient, less wasteful means of control.

As for the tawny daylilies around the reservoir, I'd had no idea that they were cultivated—in many places across the country they're considered invasive, and the way they grew upon the hill in a mad jumble, they resembled roadside weeds. Looking back on it, my guess was that at some point, long ago, someone probably *had* planted them, but that in keeping with the hardy nature of *Hemerocallis fulva*, they had escaped up and down the hill, choking out the native flora population along the way.

The commissioner's blanket example of fifteen folks gathering daylilies in one evening and decimating the entire population showed a total lack of understanding and an underestimation of the hardiness of the plant. Botanically speaking, it was hard to even make a dent in the tawny daylily population by picking their tops—*Hemerocallis fulva* propagates through underground tuberous roots, which was why it was such a successful invasive. Once established, it multiplies and spreads in thick patches, the way it had at the foot of the reservoir in Central Park. (Gardeners have a hard time weeding the plant out without digging up the entire root system, and they often inadvertently spread the plant in the process.)

Every spring since the mid-1980s, Steve Brill has led multiple tours through the area introducing would-be foragers to
the pleasures of *Hemerocallis fulva*, and despite this, the daylilies were still flourishing. In fact, it may be because of such con-
sistent foraging action that the plants were thriving. Gibbons
himself advocated digging up daylilies as a way of boosting
the plant population. ("Don't feel like a vandal while digging
daylily tubers. A spading fork full of plants removed here and
there from the clump will only give it a much-needed thinning and cultivation. If you would like to see more of these
interesting and useful plants growing, then set out some of
the plants in new places after you have removed the [edible]
tubers. They will live and each one will soon form a new colony
about itself.")

Still, despite this knowledge, I felt embarrassed, and rather
like a shamed child. How could I have missed that regulation?

That week, I called up various federal and state agencies
to see about their policies on foraging. I received conflicting
answers from the public relations officers at Gateway National
Park, the areas around the waterways in southern Queens,
Brooklyn, and Staten Island—from "take pictures, not plants"
to that they followed the National Parks Service code of regu-
lations that allowed the collection of "edible fruit, nuts, and
berries" (basically, anything that was renewable) for individual
consumption. The New York State Parks representative that I
spoke to wouldn't even tolerate the gathering of nuts or berries.
"You can't pick plants from the park!" he barked.

I contacted the public relations departments for both the
City and State's Department of Transportation—under whose
jurisdiction fell sidewalk and roadside embankments (and the
plants and fruiting trees growing along them)—but the city
agency appeared stymied by my questioning and said that

they would get back to me. (No one ever did.) I couldn't get a response from the state DOT.

Occasionally, someone (mostly online) became offended after reading about my foraging ventures. Wasn't it selfish? What if everyone did what I did—there wouldn't be anything left!

It's true that if all eight million residents decided to forage *en masse*, there would be a negative impact on the environment, but such a hypothetical seemed like hyperbole to me. In a city with so many restaurants, and where many New Yorkers complained about having so little free time, I knew that most of them were not going to expend the energy boning up on their knowledge of edible plants and mushrooms, and searching the parks for food. Not when it was so much easier to go out for dinner or order takeout.

I understood the need for preservation—preservation was what kept the city parks and green spaces safe from greedy developers. I loved preservation, and I loved the parks. Only I didn't believe that foraging, which was sustainable if practiced correctly and mindfully and which had opened my eyes to the resiliency of nature, was anti-preservation. Most foragers I knew cared about the health of the land—and protecting habitats—because it was the direct source of our food.

In parts of Europe, where foraging was an age-old tradition practiced by generations of families, the right to gather and collect edibles was protected. In Scandinavia, it fell under the principle of *Allemansrätten* or "all man's rights," aka "the right to roam," "freedom to roam," or the right to public access. *Allemansrätten* allowed for the collection of flora and fungi across Sweden, Finland, and Denmark. I had friends who grew up mushroom-hunting with their families in parts of southern Spain and Switzerland, and in southwestern France, some still practiced the traditions of *la cueillette,* the "picking" or "gathering" of wild foods such as fungi, fruit, and nuts.

A more limited version of this existed in the United Kingdom. The Theft Act of 1968 provided for gathering "flowers, fruit or foliage from a plant growing wild on any land"—even, surprisingly, on private property. So long as it wasn't for resale, and the plant wasn't within a protected class, this kind of foraging did *not* constitute theft. Some foragers referred to these as the "three Fs." Where Owen had grown up, folks gathered blackberries along ancient communal footpaths and some livestock were allowed to graze on common land.

Why didn't we have common land or provisions for the three Fs? We had a rubric of openness ("This land was made for you and me"), but when it came right down to it, most of our space was privatized—even some beaches. The only areas left for many of us were the federal, state, and city parkland. While I was heartened by the National Parks Service's allowance for the collection of "edible fruit, nuts, and berries," it still fell down to the individual parks to determine whether or not they would allow even that. I found myself longing for the kinds of rights that foragers could exercise in other parts of the world.

Later that week, Andy looked up the definition of *forage* in the *Oxford English Dictionary.*

"Food for horses and cattle," he told me over the phone. "Fodder."

But then he read the other definitions: " . . . a roving search for provisions of any kind; sometimes, a raid for ravaging the ground from which the enemy draws his supplies . . ." *To forage* meant "to collect forage from; to overrun (a country) for the purpose of obtaining or destroying supplies, to lay under contribution for forage."

"Also, in a wider sense, to plunder, pillage, ravage," he said.

I was appalled. My heart sank. To plunder, pillage, ravage? I thought *forager* had hardy connotations of going forth and finding things. Not land carnage and military takeovers.

As Andy started talking about potentially changing the column name from "Urban Forager" to something less controversial he began to sound very far away, as if he were speaking from the other end of a tunnel. (Only later did I read the *Concise Oxford English Dictionary*'s definition, "Search widely for food or provisions.")

To plunder, pillage, ravage. This wasn't what the act of foraging meant to me. I desperately wanted to change that definition, turning it on its head. If I could rewrite the meaning, it would look something like this:

Forager. Noun. One who loves the land so much that she literally eats from it.

Perhaps I would have been more upset about my morel-less hunt with the NYMS if I weren't heading out with fellow forager James Brochu, aka Puma Ghostwalker, a few days later.

It had just rained overnight, *which was really good for the morels,* Jim reminded me, especially since we were going out "on the last day of the season."

I'd first met Jim a few years ago at a local café on the north shore of Staten Island. A teacher of wild-food-survival training for the Boy Scouts, he had a booming voice and a preference for Australian-outback oilskin hats; back then, before he trimmed his mustache, he reminded me of a cross between Yosemite Sam and a bear. I didn't catch a glimpse of his tender side until much later, when he gave me a jar of wild honey from a hive that he had saved. A virulent nature-lover and orchid-tender, Jim was the kind of mycologist who, whenever he found a giant puffball that had gone past the point of being edible, would move it to another location to help spread the spores.

A week before, Jim had texted me a picture of a pile of wild morels, adding, "I think I found about 300 or more." He agreed to take me out to his newest spot, but not before first making me swear to keep the location a secret.

That morning after the rains, we were traversing a pristine area that was woody and moist, where the air smelled clean and crisp and you might never realize you were still in New York City. There was wild garlic, as tall as the stands we encountered upstate, spindly sassafras saplings, and long strands of Solomon's seal with their lovely bell-shaped flowers hanging like lacy undergarments.

"I'm taking you to one of my sweet spots," Jim said, walking ahead of me, his boots leaving deep impressions in the soil. "When you find a morel—stop, scan, and turn 360 degrees. You don't want to trample any underfoot."

After last weekend's fruitless hunt, I was eager to be in an area where the morels grew so profusely that one could trample them by accident.

We entered a clearing with full sun exposure, where the air felt wet and the loamy earth was covered in twigs, old vines, and last year's foliage. Everything was moist from the rain, which still clung to the leaves on the surrounding trees. Jim's sweet spot was the perfect combination of moisture, air circulation, brambly ground cover, and spongy soil.

"Remember—stop, look around, do a 360," Jim said, his thick hands fanning out.

I looked around, but all I saw were bramble, maple leaves, and young sprigs of mugwort.

"Oh honey, look at that," Jim said, his deep voice gone all soft and velvety, pointing to the ground about three yards away.

At first, I didn't see anything except a canvas of twisted branches and leaves. But then, there it was, under a tent of old bramble: a perfect, tan-colored morel.

Jim's face lit up, and he motioned to me to get it. I crouched down and picked the morel from its yellow base. Although hollow, it was surprisingly heavy in my hand. It smelled even better than shiitakes.

I was eager to find one of these honeycombed morels on my own without Jim's help and peered at my surroundings, squinting in the diffused sunlight.

As Jim moved on, looking for others, I felt my own frustration, built up from days of fruitless searching—now such a familiar feeling, which alternated between a rising tension and tightening in my chest and a mouthwatering hunger. I was crouched down low to the ground, sensing the morels' presence but unable to see them.

As Jim surveyed the land up ahead, I stayed behind, touching the earth, trying to gain a new perspective. I watched him growing smaller and smaller in the distance and waited for my foraging eyes to sharpen.

I was on my hands and knees, hovering above the ground, trying to meet the morels, if not at eye level and on their own terms, then at least close to it. I willed myself to breathe. Just breathe.

It was only then that I saw something, about a yard in front of me, under the cover of viney bramble, and seeming to rise up, as if in Technicolor: a beautiful, fully mature morel as large as my hand. *Morchella esculenta.* The yellow morel.

It was magical in its perfection—classically honeycombed, and vaguely leaning like the Tower of Pisa. I crawled over and inhaled its earthy aroma the way I used to when rummaging through those giant bins of mushrooms with my grandfather in Chinese supermarkets. The *Morchella* was moist and wet in my hands.

Something happens when you make your first find—it's like what people say about acid changing your vision, that once you take your first hit you never see the same way again. Once my eye and brain had the morel firmly imprinted on them from the wild, not simply in the form of an online picture or even collected in a basket, the pattern recognition really started to kick in. A few seconds later, I was able to see another, a short gray one right next to the first. And then another perfectly formed *Morchella* next to that. I was surrounded by an entire cluster of morels.

I fell back down to my knees, mushroom-drunk and giddy. I felt as if I had arrived—a full-fledged card-carrying member of the New York Mycological Society. A *real* mushroom-hunter.

I called out to Jim, who smiled and laughed at the sight of me, and then froze a second before scanning the area 360 degrees and carefully doubling back in my direction.

I was surrounded by morels—giant stands of them, growing in clumps of three and four, from tiny babies to a number that were the size of my fist. I paused a minute to acknowledge the discovery and thanked the underground mycelium, branching out in unseen threads beneath me.

We spent half an hour there, collecting as many as forty morels, before moving on to another one of Jim's "sweet spots." As my bag got heavier and heavier, more than five pounds' worth, I became almost light-headed and intoxicated, pushing past my own fatigue to look for more.

As we walked, Jim showed me spongy saffron-colored jelly mushrooms, the color of a monk's robes, growing on the bark of a downed tree. They were edible even raw, with a consistency like that of gummy bears.

And just when I thought the day couldn't get any better, we discovered another jelly fungus, layered like soft, folded ears running up and down a decaying tree trunk.

"Wood ear," Jim said. "You find it in hot and sour soup."

I stopped. Everything seemed to go out of focus for a moment, even the sound of Jim's voice, except those wood ears illuminated in the soft morning light. They were brown and nearly translucent.

Suddenly, I was remembering all of those hours eating the crunchy, related cloud ear fungus in family stir-fries, or wandering down the aisle of Chinese supermarkets with my grandparents. *What were they really? And did they grow on land or in the sea?*

Wood Ear. Tree ear. Mu'er. Mook yee. A saprophytic mushroom that grew in clusters, not just in China, where it was prized for its buoyancy and medicinal charms, but also here in my hometown, hanging off a slender tree.

Back home, the mushrooms in my bag collectively smelled like the earth, and breathing in their scent was as satisfying an olfactory experience as taking a deep whiff of a rose. I tucked the cloud ears in the refrigerator and carried the *Morchella* onto my rooftop, along with a cutting board and a paring knife, and started cleaning them out, one by one. I uncovered roly-poly bugs, tiny snails, and wispy quarter-inch worms. If these mush-rooms were purchased from a store, I'd probably be creeped out, but here their presence was living proof of the morels' connec-tion with the earth. I almost felt guilty removing them. After all, if I were a tiny creature, I would want to make my home inside a morel, too.

After an hour under the hot sun, I counted out ninety-three *Morchella esculentas* of various sizes and textures. Some morels were long and classically honeycombed, while others reminded me of rounded brain coral. I stood on my rooftop, surveying the morels before a backdrop of brownstones and skyscrapers. A mycelium or a plant, weed or otherwise, like any living thing, was imprinted with the will to live and would flourish wherever it could. Nature worked its wonders no mat-ter where we were, no matter what kinds of concrete and steel barriers or rules we tried to erect—whether it was a park or a plot of land slotted for development. I felt a sense of expan-sion, as if my heart could encompass the entire city. I thought of the natural world all around us that had given us such trea-sures, and envisioned all of the rich and earthy meals I would be able to share.

Instructions for Drying/Storing Wild Morels

I prefer this no-fuss drying method for preserving large quan-tities of morels, as it's easy and enables the *Morchella* to be stored for years. Alternatively, if one doesn't have a dehydra-tor, cooking and then freezing them is another good way of preserving a large crop.

1. Wipe away dirt or sand with fingers. Slice the mushrooms lengthwise with a paring knife. Discard any parts that are soft, mushy, or mealy when rubbed.

2. Shake out any bugs into a paper bag, bowl, or preferably, directly into the garbage. In case you are worried, I have never seen a roly-poly crawl out of a container it was tossed into (usually it crawls up into a little ball and stays there).

3. Lay out the morels onto a mesh rack and place in an area with good cross-ventilation.

4. Turn the morels over the next day for maximum air circulation. After another day or two, depending on the humidity, they should be dry enough for storage; string them up with a needle and thread to hang, or store in a plastic airtight container.

Note: Dehydrated morels can be stored for lengthy periods— I've used them after two years and they were still as aromatic and flavorful as the day I picked them, perhaps even more so. Chinese people believe that certain mushrooms, such as shiitakes, are even better dried and reconstituted, and I think that may be the case with morels.

To reconstitute, lay the dried morels in hot water, covered in a bowl, for at least five minutes. They will plump up and be soft and pliable. Save the flavorful liquid to add to sauces.

14

The Perfect Meal

Yellow Morels (*Morchella esculenta*)

Owen and I spent the next few days at his apartment, preparing for a homemade Mother's Day brunch. Lately, we had started discussing the possibilities of getting engaged and my moving in, and I thought it might be a good idea to get my mother acclimated to the idea by seeing where Owen lived, even if marriage was in the distant future.

I had prepared a simple spring menu—tomato and garlic bruschetta appetizers, and a morel and linguini pasta for the entree. I had cooked for my mother before, but never wild mushrooms, and like a good Chinese daughter, I always traveled to her home or my grandparents'.

My mother arrived in whirlwind fashion—entering the living room laden with jewelry, talking in her public school teacher's voice about how easy it was to get to the Upper East Side from her apartment and how long it had taken her to find a parking spot. Her voice seemed to fill the entire room. I used to be embarrassed about how loud she could be, but then I realized that I'd inherited the same set of vocal cords, and how handy they were in front of a classroom or when needing to catch a taxi.

She inspected the antique door handles throughout Owen's apartment and said, "You could sell those for a lot of money." She pointed to the framed map of England's southeastern coast hanging on the wall and made the same remark.

"He's not interested in selling, Ma," I said. "That's where Owen's from."

I was rather dismayed, but Owen took it all in stride, showing her around the apartment, pouring her something to drink. There wasn't time to worry about whether or not she liked the place when there was still so much to do in the kitchen, so I dashed back, trying to manage the timing of the food.

The bruschetta went out on a tray—a heaping pile of freshly chopped cherry tomatoes over toasted baguette slices rubbed with raw garlic, based on a Jamie Oliver recipe. I was still sautéing the morels and boiling the water when the tray came back empty. Owen had only a medium-size pot, which couldn't contain the volume of linguini we needed, so after the first batch was ready, I immediately started boiling more water. I served my mom and Owen first, feeling a little like a mother myself as I disappeared back into the kitchen. I kept the door open and periodically checked that their conversation was running smoothly, but all I heard was the constant stream of my mother's voice punctuated with Owen's intermittent laughter.

When I was finally able to sit down to eat at the dining room table, my mother said to Owen, "You're lucky—she can cook!"

I blushed. Owen agreed and gave me a little kiss before eating another bite.

The morels created a savory, flavorful yumminess that recalled the earth and the intense combination of springtime temperatures and moisture that had gone into their creation. Combined with the butter, shallots, and cream sherry, it was a rich, umami experience twirled around the tines of my fork.

"Happy Mother's Day," I said, lifting my glass, suddenly inspired.

"You should have made more," my mother said, finishing her last mouthful, "for me to take home."

I was so surprised by her remark that for several seconds, all I could do was focus on the necklaces adorning her neck—two fanciful, filigreed antique necklaces adorned with angels and flowers. She was trying to give a kind of backhanded, Chinese compliment. *I liked it so much, I wish you would have made me more.*

But the comment felt particularly sharp and critical, and not just because of all my efforts in the kitchen and out in the field foraging. It was a little like the days after Grandma died, when I felt as if nothing I did was good enough, and all I could do was take motherwort to dull the pain.

So the comment hung in the air, while I sat there stymied over what to say.

Owen, who was gobbling up the food, continued eating.

When I was a kid living in Queens, before the boyfriends and the disappointments and my own dating history, I thought my mother was a kind of superwoman. For years, she traveled out to an inner-city elementary school in Bushwick, Brooklyn, teaching third-graders math, reading, and science, despite the innumerable times her car was broken into, and despite being assaulted by a student from another class. She was a formidable teacher whom her kids respected, and one day one of her students told me, "I like Ms. Chin—she's nice, but very strict."

She held our small family together on her teacher's salary, and even though we never took vacations—my mom preferred to spend her summers at home reading Jane Austen novels with me at the occasional day camp—there were always flea markets and antique shows upstate or down in the Village to occupy our afternoons.

Most of my friends found her young and fascinating, with her love of R&B and her knowledge of what was hip and fashionable. She wasn't like other people's parents—many of whom were hardworking immigrants who had married their childhood sweetheart or the person their families had chosen for them. The fact that my mother was young and divorced was hyper-cool and über-American. She could dance. She drove a stick-shift sports car.

They didn't seem to mind her dating as much as I did. "That's your mother's boyfriend?" one classmate gushed after meeting the baby-faced bartender whom I'd resented the most. "He's totally hot!"

My mother took issue over the superwoman characterization. "I can't live up to that," she told me one day. "I know you expect me to be everything, but I'm not."

But I knew she was wrong. Back then, she *was* my everything, and she certainly appeared as if she could deflect bullets with just a sweep of her black hair or a sidelong glance.

Long after my mother returned home to Flushing, and Owen and I had cleared the few leftovers from our Mother's Day meal off the table, I entered Owen's kitchen exhausted. I wanted to crawl into bed, but I still had about a dozen fresh morels remaining that were too valuable to let spoil. Jason Cortlund from the NYMS had told me that morels preserved well after being cooked and immediately frozen, so I set about prepping them for the pan again.

As I cleaned and sliced through the *Morchella* crosswise, so that they piled up on the chopping board resembling little tasty cogs, I thought about why I had felt so hurt by my mother's remark. Many women I knew were sensitive to their mother's comments, and it was a common complaint from mothers that they couldn't tell their daughters anything. But it wasn't just that. While I had given up on Stanley a long time ago, I was still holding out for some kind of change with her. And now with both grandparents gone, there was only us.

I added the morels to the hot pan, watching them shrink and dance in the bubbling butter. I thought about all the years of guilt I'd felt over my father walking out. The unspoken belief that I'd been the one who ruined my mother's life. I had so desperately wanted us to have a better relationship—the kind of bond that I'd had with my grandmother—that it completely blinded me from seeing my mother for who she really was.

In some way, I had wanted her to treat me with the same love and care that my grandmother had. As I tossed the morels so that they began to brown on both sides, and the room became infused with the fragrance of buttery mushrooms, I slowly became aware of my mistake. To expect my mother to be anything or in any way different from who she was would be a fallacy. Like attempting to find wild morels growing in a place and season contrary to their nature.

I looked down at the mass of morels sizzling in the pan. It was mid-May, and in Boulder, Colorado, this season's crop of motherwort would be flourishing under a hot Rocky Mountain sun; in a few weeks across the five boroughs, the mulberries would be hanging off so many *Morus* trees. Even though the season for fruiting seemed so short and ephemeral, I knew that the skillset for finding what was available—versus what I was so ardently wishing for—was just a matter of a little knowledge, timing, and the right perspective and foraging eyes.

Suddenly, I was reminded of the lessons that a simple garlic mustard rosette had taught me: To really know something, whether it was a plant or a loved one, was to see it in all of its different stages—from seed to sprout to summertime flowering, and then on to autumn and eventually winter maturity. I had known my mother only while growing up, in the wake of my father and then all of the boyfriends, just as she was trying to put the pieces back together. Perhaps it was time to see her, to see us, as we really were, coping and thriving in the wilderness of the city.

Wild Morel Linguini

1 garlic clove, minced

1 tablespoon butter

2 small shallots, diced

8 ounces sliced morels

1 tablespoon cream sherry

1 tablespoon heavy cream

salt and pepper, to taste

1 pound cooked linguini

1 teaspoon extra virgin olive oil

>> **Yield: 4 servings**

1. Sauté the garlic in the butter over medium heat, then add the shallots; cook until garlic is slightly browned around the edges and shallots turn translucent.

2. Add the sliced chopped morels and cook until they are a deep chocolaty color.

3. Drizzle in the cream sherry—my grandfather always favored Harvey's Bristol Cream, and I follow in the tradition. Allow everything to simmer for 10 minutes.

4. Remove from the heat, and finish the sauce off with a touch of heavy cream and salt and pepper to taste.

5. Add the linguini to the sauce; toss with tongs until the morel sauce has been evenly worked through the pasta. Drizzle in the extra virgin olive oil.

15

The Queen

Honeybees (*Apis mellifera*)

By the end of the spring semester, Owen had been my unofficial photographer and foraging partner for going on seven months. He helped with everything from tasting pokeweed shoots I'd forced from their roots—shoots that made our mouths tingle—to gathering and transforming dandelion blossoms into a honey-like jelly and a home-brewed wine. But while our foraging life was growing lusher with every season, I was feeling completely stymied by Owen's divorce. Even though he had been separated from his wife in Berlin for more than a year, they were no nearer to divorcing than when we'd first met. I was already falling deeply in love with Owen, and it was clear that he felt the same way about me, but his still being married made me feel vulnerable, as though everything could shift like a sudden change in the weather.

I was walking across campus after an angry phone conversation with him over why things were still dragging on, when something soft and light as a cotton ball hit me in the face.

I waved it away, distractedly, until another one hit me on the forehead. When I looked up, the swirling commotion above me made it appear as if the sky had darkened. It took me a moment to realize that I'd walked into a giant, buzzing swarm of bees.

Another professor several yards ahead stopped and turned. "What are they?" he asked, as the insects made drunken patterns in the air.

"Bees," I murmured. There must have been tens of thousands of them. We paused for several moments, just staring at the swarm that had taken over a section of the quad. Two undergraduates behind us stopped talking and stared as well.

I fumbled for my phone to call Jim Brochu. Jim had been keeping honeybees for years, even though it had only recently been legalized in the city. In his job as a tree surgeon, he'd often come across feral hives, which he would transport to hive boxes he had tucked away in secret locations. Jim and I had just been texting that morning about Staten Island's decimated bee population. ("Another dead wild bee hive. That's five this year," he texted me from his mobile phone. "This is a HUGE problem.")

"I'm in the middle of a swarm of bees," I said when Jim picked up, a bee flying by my ear so closely, I could almost feel its wings. "You want to come and get them?"

"Have they settled?"

"They're swirling around. It's like *Day of the Locust*, only pleasant."

"They're totally docile and love-drunk on pheromones," Jim said, his voice getting all moist and faraway-sounding. "I envy you, experiencing your very first swarm. Call me when they've settled on one spot."

I hung up and watched the bees. I didn't know how long it would take for them to settle down, but the whole experience was heady, like studying fireflies at dusk.

When I returned to the site fifteen minutes later, the swarm had landed in three clumps onto a small dawn redwood tree on the quad's edge.

Although a few passersby stared, most just kept walking. They were lost in their own thoughts, as I had been only moments earlier.

I redialed Jim. "It's happening—Come as soon as you can."

For the past few years, I had been reading articles on the decline of the global bee population and a syndrome called colony collapse disorder (CCD), in which entire populations of honeybees were disappearing without a trace. In a recent survey of American hives, the Apiary Inspectors of America reported that U.S. hives had experienced a terrifying 33.8 percent population drop in just that past year alone (this, on top of several years of steady decreases). The report coincided with what Jim and others had witnessed firsthand in New York City—thousands of bees mysteriously vanishing from their hives, leaving behind only the queen and her defenseless brood. With the global bee population already on a decline, this newest phenomenon had left scientists stymied and scrambling for answers.

In light of this global phenomenon, it seemed even more important for us to save the swarm.

I rushed into my department office, where I enlisted the help of our secretary to find out how we could relocate the bees.

"If you want to do that," Wendy said slowly, letting the request settle in, "why not go to the top?"

She gave me the information on a VP who could help.

After messaging him, I called Andy. "I just encountered a swarm of bees on campus. You want this story?"

I was reading up on swarming—a natural phenomenon that occurred, usually in the spring, whenever a colony grew too large—when Jim sent me a message saying he would be there within the hour.

We'd gotten official permission to relocate the honeybees, and I was happily printing out legal forms, when it occurred to me that I probably wasn't the only one who'd witnessed the swarm.

I ran back into the office and had Wendy call security. But the guard on duty already knew about the bees.

"They called the exterminator twenty minutes ago," she said. "The guy's already on his way."

I ran out the door, ready to throw myself between the bees and the exterminator if need be.

Got to save the bees, I thought, bursting through the doors.

Whenever *Apis mellifera* hit a certain population size, a large portion of the colony would make preparations to leave, but only after the queen gave birth to a new virgin queen. This natural order of growth and succession gave rise to a truism I was to hear from bee experts in interview after interview: *There can be only one queen.*

While the swarm waited in a temporary place, usually not too far from the original hive, individual scouts searched for a new home. If successful, they persuaded the entire swarm to travel with them in a buzzing dance called a waggle; this heavily democratic process with thousands of bees weighing in could take several hours or even days. Although harmless, many city folks new to the experience found the sight of a giant flash mob of bees unusual and rather alarming.

By the time I arrived, the bees had shifted again, this time in two long, vertical clumps along separate branches. They were so alive and heavy that they dragged the branches down like twigs, and were starting to combine at the bottom. Collectively swarming over one another in a frantic effort to protect the queen, the honeybees appeared to be dripping like succulent meat turning on a spit. There were too many to discern who was waggling versus who was simply taking part in the general busyness of bee activity.

I was panting, glad that I wouldn't have to wrestle some exterminator to the ground or tie myself to the tree to make a point.

Ten minutes later, Jim arrived in his Dodge Durango— looking like the outdoorsy Vietnam War veteran that he was with his graying Yosemite Sam mustache and wraparound sunglasses. No one would have guessed from his hat and work boots that Jim was a self-styled nature photographer who regularly read Pema Chödrön. "Hello, darlin'," he said, smiling at me through the opened window.

By the time we'd parked and returned to the bees, the swarm had transformed into a giant three-foot-long teardrop.

"Oh my God," Jim said, his mouth dropping open. "That's thirty thousand bees."

Jim had a smaller bee suit for me, which resembled a hazmat suit. As I zipped it up, he helped me adjust my mask. Through the mesh screen, I could see his big, bushy mustache. "It's like it was made for you," he murmured.

I was safely covered up, donning thick yellow gloves as heavy as oven mitts, when I realized that we'd attracted a bit of a gathering. The campus lawyer was there, along with a few curious students, as well as the school's publicist, with a video camera. Jim seemed to puff up in front of an audience.

"Do you have allergies?" Jim asked me, stepping into his suit.

"To pine nuts," I said, not mentioning that my mosquito bites sometimes swelled to the circumference of tennis balls. "I don't know if I'm allergic to beestings or not."

"I have an EpiPen," one of the student onlookers offered.

All zipped up, Jim and I approached the bees. It was a little like stepping into a noisy construction zone—the closer we got, the louder and more frenetic the bees seemed to become. Bees were everywhere: landing on my facial netting, the front of my suit, and all across my shoulders. The back of Jim's head mask had become a landing strip. I might have been more afraid of getting stung if I weren't aware of the fact that the entire colony was at stake. So I stayed steady, watching the bees' almost liquid movements undulate across the branch.

As Jim worked on placing the carrier bucket as close as he could underneath the swarm, I held the saw and the lid. The sounds of my own breathing mixed in with the nearly deafening buzzing of the honeybees. I rather expected to be descended upon by freaked-out workers in attack mode, but the swarms really were docile, even this close-up. I handed Jim the saw, and in one unbelievably swift motion, he cut through the branches and lowered the entire swarm into the waiting bucket.

There was an almost collective sigh as I closed the lid, and our gang of onlookers came forward to take a closer look. Ken, the publicist, held the flip camera out in one hand, as Jim started getting into describing the nitty-gritty of swarming, really hamming it up for the video.

"The workers and drones gorge themselves on honey," he said, using his hands like goal posts to frame his face for emphasis. "And then they take off, and they swarm, and they fly around the queen." Jim worked his arms as if he had an invisible lasso above his head. "And they get together and they converge . . . and they make this ball, and the queen will be in the center."

As I handed the paperwork over to the lawyer, I could hear Jim's resonant voice growing louder.

"In a world population of almost seven billion people, the earth cannot sustain that many people," he said, staring intently into the camera as several remaining bees flew past his head. "So with our massive agriculture, truckloads of bees come in and pollinate corn and wheat and soy, by the hundreds of millions of bees.

"If we lose them, we lose those crops, and people could go hungry"—said Jim before hesitating—"in about a day or two."

Sadly, a few hundred bees still circled around us, gathering along the trunk of the tree.

"What'll happen to them?" I asked.

"They'll either return to the old hive," Jim said, "or they'll die."

As the small crowd dispersed, we walked toward the car carrying the buzzing bucket, Jim speculating that the original hive was probably living in the woodland that abutted the campus. He placed the bees in the backseat, and we headed off—to a wooded area where Jim stashed his hive boxes—while the honeybees buzzed in the back of the car and the wind blew through my hair.

We arrived fifteen minutes later, making our way on foot through a dense copse of trees. Jim recounted the eight hives he'd lost to CCD. The bees were at risk on an epic scale, he said, leaving beekeepers across the country to point their fingers at pesticides, parasitic mites, even cell phone towers.

"Do you think that cell phone towers have anything to do with it?" I asked him doubtfully.

"Probably not," Jim said. "After all, we were using some pretty gnarly stuff back in the 1960s."

I thought of Rachel Carson's *Silent Spring* as I scrambled to keep up across the uneven terrain.

Jim's hive box was an old white thing the size of a building air-conditioning unit, hidden behind wild garlic mustard overgrowth and several branches. Its former inhabitants—a feral colony he'd saved after a storm knocked down a giant hardwood tree—had disappeared earlier that year. I watched, chewing on some young garlic mustard leaves, as Jim dismantled the entire box, which, with its dangling frames, resembled a giant, wooden file folder.

We divvied up the load, with Jim taking the majority of the components. Jim hoisted the foundation and several of the wooden hive bodies—rectangular boxes from which the moveable frames were suspended—within his arms, and I followed behind with the remaining parts. Although I was carrying significantly less, I struggled with it through the woods, nearly tripping on tree roots, watching Jim's broad back navigating the rough terrain. He was so amazingly light-footed that he appeared to almost be dancing, which mystified me, given the weight of the objects he was carrying. I tried to keep up, but I kept getting whacked in the face by tree branches.

Midway through, Jim stopped and regarded me, as I nearly dropped what I was carrying. I felt like an idiot weakling, especially when Jim insisted that I place some of my load on top of his before continuing onward. But I followed him more easily this time, only occasionally stumbling.

Back at Jim's place on the South Shore, we got to work setting up the hive box in a field of mugwort and tall grasses.

"I've been waiting a long time for something like this," he said, first laying down a wooden pallet and then the hive foundation. Jim had saved a number of wild hives before, but never an entire swarm facing extermination.

He faced the hive entrance south for maximum sunlight, and whacked the debris off each honeycomb frame before placing it into the box. After I cleared some of the mugwort away, the hive, now two stacks high and large enough to house the entire colony, was ready. We donned our bee suits and got to work.

Jim slowly peeled back the carrier lid, revealing a mass of bees resembling a long triangular beard. Their insistent buzzing was almost comforting. As Jim carefully tipped them into the waiting box below, trying not to injure a single worker, I couldn't help but wonder about the queen. Where was she among the workers and the male drones? What did she look like with her juicy, egg-filled abdomen? I couldn't see her beyond the throngs of worker bees, but I knew she was there in the middle, as if some centrifugal force were drawing everything to her.

It was getting dark, and Jim placed the lid back on the hive box. We watched the remaining hundred bees outside the entrance wobble around in confusion, crawling among the mugwort. "They'll settle and hopefully take to their new surroundings," said Jim.

In the fading light, we sat and talked, hoping that the bees would like their new home, pondering what would have happened if the exterminator had arrived before we did. It was dusk when we finally saw the powers of the queen at work. The remaining honeybees filed in through the hive entrance four to five in a row, like theatergoers receiving the call that intermission is over, moving quickly into their new home.

The next day, I phoned Dr. Diana Cox-Foster, a leading entomologist at Pennsylvania State University who was trying to uncover the causes of honeybee decline. Each winter for the past few years, one in every three colonies across the country failed and died. Talking to me from her office, Cox-Foster listed a range of problems facing *Apis mellifera*, including parasitic mites, loss of natural habitat, and a mono-diet (commercial bees trucked in to pollinate single crops didn't obtain the range of food they needed). Most suspicious and alarming, she said, was the sudden increase in pesticides found within hives.

"Bees are being exposed to many more pesticides in greater significant amounts than we ever anticipated," Dr. Cox-Foster said. Researchers found on average eight different kinds of herbicides and fungicides in pollen samples, including DDT, which was banned in 1972.

"Our ecosystems depend upon pollinators and flowering plants," she said. "If you remove them, everything might fall down."

I asked her what ordinary folks could do.

"Plant more bee-friendly plants and decrease pesticide use," she said. "Many pesticides that are found in lawn and garden centers are the same ones that are used in our agricultural fields."

I had honeybees on the brain for the next several days—even to the point of hearing their buzzing in my head before I went to bed. The more I read about *Apis mellifera* in James and Carol Gould's *The Honey Bee*, the more intriguing they became for me—a matriarchal society, with a dominant female population, where the male drones were tolerated for the sole purpose of mating with the queen (and then unceremoniously cast off when no longer needed). They were the Amazon women of the insect world.

And then there was her royal highness herself. Reared on royal jelly, the queen was not only gigantic, but under normal conditions, the sole bee endowed with the ability to lay eggs—upward of two thousand a day. She could sting without it being fatal to her, and when still just a young virgin, she had killed off any emerging sister queens before they could usurp her. Her powerful pheromones repressed the ovary development of her workers, attracted the care and attention of special nurse bees that attended her every need, and inhibited the production of new queens until the timing was right for the swarming to begin.

In the late spring, as the weather warmed up and a new batch of young queen larvae was being reared, the queen herself consumed a thinning diet that enabled her to become svelte enough for flight. After releasing pheromones that made the workers love-drunk and docile, the queen gave the signal and flew out of the hive—and in one glorious, almost symphonic movement, the majority of the colony flew after her.

Owen called later that night as I was studying photographs of our bee rescue. "What would you like to do this weekend?"

I looked at the open picture on my computer: I was in the background, cautiously circling the mass of bees at a respectful distance. The photograph was taken before I'd ever donned a

bee suit and knew anything about honeybee behavior and society. *There can be only one queen.*

"I'd love to see you," I said, finally. "But I'm afraid that I'm
busy."

I headed out for Jim's a few days later. The honeybee rescue
story was slotted for that Sunday's paper and I couldn't wait to
check up on our bees.

When I arrived that afternoon, dozens of honeybees were
hovering around the hive box. Some were alighting on the
wood entrance with pollen coating their legs like saffron leg
warmers. Others were heavy with nectar. Each one was immediately sniffed at by guard bees, to make sure they were a part of
the colony, before being allowed to disappear into the darkness
of the hive.

Jim approached the hive box in his suit and heavy gloves,
using slow and methodical movements before taking off the
lid. The bees were a mass of activity and buzzing loudly, crawling over one another, a rippling lake of insects across the entire
hive body, some laying pin-size slivers of wax from their abdo-
mens, their wings translucent in the light. Over the course
of just a few days, the bees had been busy laying honeycomb,
even across a few of the frames, effectively blocking them. Jim
pried the wax off with a hive tool the length of his forearm and
handed it to me.

"It's been mathematically proven that honeycomb is the
most efficient structure for a colony," Jim said, tilting a frame
in my direction. It was a sheet of nearly perfect hexagonal
cells whose symmetry made my breath catch. (Darwin, studying honeybees for his theory of natural selection, marveled at

such architecture, calling it "absolutely perfect in economizing labour and wax.")

I peered closer into the hive box, watching worker upon worker scurry over one another in a mad, undulating ripple. I could just make out the spare drones from the tireless female workers, but it was still impossible for me to discern the queen. I knew she was there, though, evident in every movement of the colony.

By now, several more dozens of bees were arriving and setting off from the hive. We were in prime foraging season for *Apis mellifera*, where current gains could offset future losses in colder months. There was an old English saying, "A swarm in May is worth a load of hay, a swarm in June is worth a silver spoon, but a swarm in July isn't worth a fly." A late-swarming colony, not having had enough time to build adequate honey stores, wouldn't survive the winter. Our swarm, as we kept our fingers crossed, just might.

Jim placed the lid back onto the hive and we removed our bee suits. I sat back on my heels at a respectful distance and studied the cream-colored honeycomb that the bees had built like a bridge between the frames. It was still warm in my hands and shaped like the starship *Enterprise*.

It took a cast of thousands to support a queen, and in turn, a queen to lead a colony of bees. Neither could exist without the other. Even the lazy drones, those daft playthings, had their usefulness. Every entity within the hive was a co-conspirator in this never-ending cycle of foraging and building, of honey production and comb creation. Like the fungi locked in a symbiotic relationship with the very roots and soil of trees and plants surrounding it, sprouting morels and reishis and cloud ear mushrooms, everything was interconnected, interrelated, and interdependent.

As I watched the frenetic activity of the honeybees, I thought of the people who raised me—my grandparents, my mother, even the specter of my father—as well as the circumstances that had formed like honeycomb all around us. I thought of Owen locked in his divorce struggle with his wife in Berlin. Even on our very worst days, none of us was acting alone. All of the forces of nature driving all of life itself were here, presenting and working around us. And nothing, not a single thing, was standing still.

Wild Honey & Parmesan Cracker Drizzles

If I don't have a lot of time but I still want to impress my guests, this is my go-to hors d'oeuvre. Any quality hard cheese will do, but I am partial to the way that a good Parmesan, with its salty nuttiness, marries with the flavor of wild honey. Tip: They say that the darker the honey, the deeper the flavor, so use the darkest local honey that you can find.

> 5-ounce box of crackers
> 8-ounce block of Parmesan cheese
> 4 tablespoons or $^1/_4$ cup wild or local honey

Arrange the crackers on a serving platter. Cut the Parmesan into $^1/_8$-inch slices, and then place the cheese on the crackers. With a spoon, drizzle the honey over each cheese cracker. Wild honey is so flavorful that a little goes a long way. For fun, practice writing the first initial of your name in honey over each cracker.

16

When Food Was Food

I'd better get my act together," Owen said, after I told him about how Jim and I had saved the bees, and then, a week later, how we rescued a doe trapped in a nearby ditch. "Before you run away with Crocodile Dundee."

From that day forward and throughout the rest of the summer, while Owen worked on his divorce, my productivity was nearly on the level of the honeybees. I covered flora and even some local fauna across neighborhoods throughout the city, including a *Cannabis sativa* plant growing in front of a bus stop in Ditmas Park, its heavy fragrance lingering in my nose after I'd pinched a leaf with my fingers; a female European green crab only slightly larger than my thumb, which I caught in the salty waters of Jamaica Bay; wild purslane, which I'd found growing on my doctor's lawn on Staten Island, then pickled and served as a side dish; a baby lion's mane jellyfish swimming in the Gowanus Canal—a sign the former industrial wasteland

and newly designated Superfund site was getting healthier; and jimsonweed—a harrowingly hallucinogenic plant referred to in Haiti as "zombie cucumber"—growing around the corner from my writing studio (just inhaling its tahini-like scent gave me bad dreams).

I led a series of foraging tours through Fort Greene and Prospect Park—doing it as an ad-hoc guerrilla foraging venture, where I pointed out plantain and dandelion rosettes growing through cracks in the sidewalks and showed folks the best areas to find lambsquarters in the park, growing to the height of my chest. I deepened my connection with the Brooklyn Botanic Garden, whose experts helped me to identify the different species of mulberry trees and blackberry varieties I found across the city, and wrote my first foraging story for a glossy food magazine.

Foraging was becoming a hot topic in the media, and I was approached about appearing as an expert on radio and television programs, including one on WNYC, my local NPR affiliate.

Although the TV segments went nowhere—most of the producers I'd spoken to wanted to cut corners and "plant" a variety of edibles near one another to minimize travel and shooting time, which I was not willing to do—I spoke to reporters from print publications, including *Time* and AOL's *Daily Finance*. *Why are people doing it?* they wanted to know. *Where do you do it? And what kinds of things can you get?*

While some people like Steve Brill ran tours and charged a nominal fee, and intrepid young foragers like Iso Rabins out in San Francisco concocted wild food parties and sold shares of boxed wild edibles, I talked about the hidden foragers— those immigrant grandmotherly types I'd encountered in Fort Greene and Prospect parks practicing the foraging habits of their homelands. They, and we, were engaging in a kind of pre-agricultural endeavor that kept us tied close to the land. It wasn't such an odd thing in other parts of the world—I knew of Russian, Korean, and French foragers who grew up gathering edibles with their families. (One young woman, whom I met during a Brooklyn jam-making session, collected dandelion blossoms with her grandmother on the outskirts of Moscow.) Even Chef René Redzepi regularly foraged along the Danish coastline for his Copenhagen restaurant Noma, often named the "Best Restaurant in the World."

Ever since the United States had lost its foraging culture by forcing Native Americans off the land, and food was subsequently taken over by big agribusiness, most Americans that I talked to were suspicious of any food that didn't come prepackaged from a store. I had friends who visibly winced after I told them what I did, and more than one asked, "How do you know it's safe?" (Even though I explained how I foraged in areas away from cars and pollution, and how wild greens were more nutritious than their overbred cultivated cousins because they had to defend themselves against more rigorous environmental factors—those phytochemicals were actually good for us—they were still dubious.)

But things were slowly starting to change. I'd met freegans committed to living off the food grid, foodies and chefs interested in finding wild mushrooms or sweet summer berries, and yoga practitioners and Slow Foods types who had read Gary Nabhan's *Coming Home to Eat*, Barbara Kingsolver's *Animal, Vegetable, Miracle*, and anything by Michael Pollan they could get their hands on. Nearly everyone I spoke to was suspicious of big agriculture and genetically modified foods. Most were eager to return to the days when food was food, without a long list of additives and preservatives.

❦

I was talking on the phone to a producer for public radio several days before I was going to appear on a segment to discuss wild foods. I was standing in my bedroom, watching the squirrels scrambling along the tree branches outside my window. The producer had just asked me why I started foraging.

I hesitated for a moment. Unlike many of the other foraging experts I knew, I realized that I had entirely personal reasons for doing it.

"Foraging reminds me that the world is a generous place," I said. "Even when things are topsy-turvy, I know that the plants will always sprout in the spring, become lush in the summer, and then grow dormant in the winter. And the following year, it'll happen all over again."

After we wrapped up the interview, I remained by my window, overlooking the brownstone roof decks and backyards. As my eye followed a squirrel racing along a tree branch, suddenly it was as if I were seeing it for the very first time. I noted the varied leaves, the tree's height (nearly three stories high), and the profusion of garnet-colored berries. I knew that if I could stick my head out and reach my nose under the shade of that tree I would smell its fermenting, wine-like scent. *Morus rubra. Mulberries.*

I thought of all that time last year spent searching for a mulberry tree as my grandmother lay dying, when there it was all along, fruiting outside my bedroom window.

❦

A few days later, I received the following email from Eli in Boulder:

Hey Ava,

How are you doing? What's new in your life? How is your foraging going? How is teaching? How is Brooklyn? How's your family? Is there anyone special in your life now?

I think I have had a very good year out here so far. I really like where I live off an "offbeat street" but totally convenient to everything. There are events/outdoor bands in downtown Boulder and I am doing a little volunteering in the community.

Last weekend, I cycled to a friend's 20 miles away—totally "banal" route by Boulder standards, but beautiful, with bike lanes everywhere and generally very courteous drivers. On the 4th of July, I cycled a far distance to a lake and I think we saw more bikes than cars (definitely more horses/cows/goats/buffaloes than cars :)). One pickup that drove by us had a bicycle and BBQ in back . . .

Attached are a few pics of me cycling as part of a week-long tour between towns in southern Colorado/Chama, New Mexico. During the first day I got myself up Slumgullian pass after cycling 60 miles uphill to get there!

Love, Eli

In the photographs, Eli and his friends were sporting skin-tight biking outfits with funny aerodynamic goggles and head-gear, posing with their bikes in front of amazing vistas and land formations. They looked adorably goofy and earnest.

But my favorite one was of Eli standing alone on a 10,000-foot summit, the windswept mountains and cumulus clouds behind him, raising his bike above his head in a victory salute, looking like he had finally arrived.

FALL

17

A Wild Tart

Oyster mushrooms (*Pleurotus ostreatus*)

I am standing on a busy closed-off avenue in Clinton Hill, participating in the Brooklyn Food Coalition's Good Food Fest—an event that's part street fair and part educational food opportunity for local artisans, foodistas, chefs, and urban farmers. All afternoon, I've been watching demonstrations from local chefs, bakers, and beekeepers, including folks from Growing Chefs, Eagle Street Rooftop Farm, and the NYC Beekeeping Meetup. This is my first cooking competition, and the dish that has taken me hours to prepare is safely tucked away in a ceramic baking dish under a cotton kitchen cloth. A small crowd has started gathering around our table, despite the presence of darkening rain clouds.

I'm wedged between an aspiring caterer with a salmon-and-capers dish and an Asian American home cook who's about to start demonstrating his peanut noodle mixing technique in front of a giant bin of long noodles. A latecomer, Rachael Mamane, the owner of Brooklyn Bouillon, a sustainably produced stock and demi-glace company, comes rushing up to enter her paella, which I had just tasted a half hour earlier. Rachael's cooking is artful and delicious. I'm not worried about the salmon woman or the peanut noodle guy, but I *am* nervous about Rachael, who is the chef for her own seasonal supper club. As she starts to lay out her food in equal piles of seafood and rice for the judges, I look down at my entry, which is as large as my two outspread hands.

I know that setting one's heart on winning something is a surefire way to set oneself up for failure. But I really, really want to win this food competition. I want to win so much that it's embarrassing. So I keep this information to myself, not even admitting it to Owen, who is standing at the other end of the table.

Judging today's competition is a panel of "celebrity judges" including the national director of Meatless Mondays, a *Huffington Post* writer, a professional baker, and a representative from the local city council office. Originally, there were going to be prizes in multiple categories, but instead, the organizers have decided to award the top three entries.

We are told to write out a list of the ingredients on a paper plate and leave it by our dishes. I'm handed a purple marker and try to write as legibly as possible:

"Urban Forager" Oyster Mushroom–Fig–Goat Cheese Tart with Caramelized Onions:

Oyster mushrooms (Prospect Park)
Figs (Fort Greene)
Goat cheese (Vermont)
Wild yeast pastry dough (Park Slope)

As I finish writing, it begins to rain.

A month before, I'd received an emailed flyer from friends that the Brooklyn Food Coalition (BFC), an offshoot of the Park Slope Food Coop, was planning a food contest in conjunction with its Good Food Fest. I'd been following the BFC ever since it started some years back, with its mission to promote access to healthy, sustainable food for everyone—especially within our most disenfranchised neighborhoods. The flyer read:

Call for Chefs, Gardeners, Canning, Beekeeping Experts and All Things 'Food & Green'

We're looking for New York City's most innovative and courageous home chefs, cooking contestants, food artisans, gardeners, canning, beekeeping and other DIY food & gardening experts to participate in the Brooklyn Food Coalition's GOOD FOOD FEST.

*Best dish contestants – Enter a dish for a chance to win. Celebrity judges will award grand prizes for "tastiest," "healthiest," "greenest," and "largest" dish!

Some months back, I had been approached by chef and cookbook author Louisa Shafia (*Lucid Food*) to throw a wild foods dinner, which, because of our schedules and timing, we had never been able to get off the ground. I still loved the idea, but was nervous to do anything on that scale on my own. A single dish, though—that was within the realm of possibility.

Since it had been such a hit at my wild foods brunch, I planned on creating an early autumnal version of that savory wild greens pie, using lambsquarters as the star ingredient. I was kind of in love with the dish's versatility, which easily accommodated a rotating roster of seasonal ingredients. Plus, how could I go wrong with Gruyère and grass-fed ricotta cheese?

Days before the competition, I set out early into the park, feeling a heightened sense of excitement as I hiked across familiar terrain. It was warm even here under the cover of tall trees—the kind of morning where everything was covered in a layer of moisture that made it feel more like late August than early September. There were no offerings under the red oak tree, but instead, strands of burgundy-tinged Virginia creeper crawling up its trunk. Through the dense foliage, I could make out cyclists and runners jogging down below, but I knew that unless any of them looked up, which they rarely did, I was largely hidden from view.

I reached the top of Lambsquarters Hill, expecting to find stands of fresh *Chenopodium album* in all its glory as I had some weeks before, but soon discovered that the plants had gone almost completely and utterly to seed. Underneath them, the dark green leaves were tough, dry, and tasteless. Two years ago, I would have spat the leaf out onto the ground. Today, I swallowed.

I walked back empty-handed, down the hill and back through the wooded area, the flavor of disappointment once again heavy in my mouth.

The only difference now was that I knew such things were temporary. The weight I now carried was largely from the items in my bag, including my worn copy of Gibbons's *Stalking the Wild Asparagus.*

In many ways, perhaps I was the perfect person to become a forager. What had started with the search for my father was soon followed up by all those years yearning for a real love to fulfill me. It was only until I started looking for my own food, getting to know the edible plants and mushrooms all around me, that I had started to understand that everything in nature was cyclical, everything interrelated. And the timing of things was key. Like footsteps visible within frost and mud, my path as a forager led me through different neighborhoods throughout the city, through parks and streets and abandoned lots, all the way up to where I was now, among the maples and the oaks, where the tulip poplar saplings and the wood sorrel thrived, where the reishi mushrooms bloomed across decaying logs. Instead of wishing for something or someone to be there that wasn't, I could now see clearly before me what was.

The false Solomon's seal, thick as a carpet, starting to bear fruit.

A reddish stalk of pokeweed, heavy with a profusion of blacker-than-black berries, tipping back toward the ground.

Somewhere in the woods, a cicada, humming like it was the height of summer.

Suddenly, I was smelling the wet, wet scent of mushrooms lingering in the air.

And there it was, growing on a stories-high tree, just out of reach: a collection of the freshest, prettiest oyster mushrooms I had ever seen. *Pleurotus ostreatus.* Creamy white, they fanned out in a giant cluster across the tree trunk like a bride's bouquet.

And there, several yards away, across the leafy terrain, a log, a foothold, ready to be rolled.

I could just about visualize the fungi's plume of whitish-lavender spores raining down, enveloping me in its cool embrace. If I died at that moment, and all the right conditions of wind, moisture, spores, and trees came together, I might someday sprout cascades of oyster mushrooms from my arms and hands and lips—enough oysters to feed thousands.

I crouched down and rolled the log with my bare hands until it rested against the base of the tree.

No matter where I was, nature would always find a way to flourish. I drew comfort in that, knowing that I was home.

I stood in my kitchen staring at the pale, tender folds of *Pleurotus ostreatus* taking over my countertop. There were more than two pounds of it, sweet-smelling like Japanese erasers, and I was giddy with pleasure. I was happily slicing into a few with a paring knife when I remembered something.

I hated oyster mushrooms. Whenever I ordered them at restaurants, they were always disappointingly slimy.

I hated oyster mushrooms.

What the hell was I going to do?

I could feel myself going into full-on, heart-thumping freakout mode—how was I going to pull off this food contest with slimy mushrooms?—until I remembered that I had resources, i.e., friends at the New York Mycological Society. Filmmaker Jason Cortlund was about to start production of his feature film *Now, Forager,* but not so busy he couldn't pass along the following culinary tip when I called him on the phone: *roast the sliced oysters until they have browned and caramelized.*

Fifteen minutes later, I was pulling the oyster mushrooms out of the oven, where they had shrunk down to about half their size, under a touch of extra virgin olive oil and salt and pepper. Roasted and smolderingly golden, the mushrooms were a revelation. Any hint of slime was removed by the dry heat, revealing a chewy meatiness like choice abalone. (I grew up eating my grandfather's braised abalone as a kid, and I loved tearing my teeth into its chewy umami-ness.) These oysters were so addictively tasty that I had to stop myself from gobbling up every tender morsel.

I assessed my kitchen and "pantry"—a highboy shelving unit for china that now displayed wild jams and dried mushrooms. I wanted to create something wild, something stunning, and a pasta or linguini dish just wouldn't do. Luckily, there was my wild yeast "mother," created from a batch of staghorn sumac berries, flour, and water, which Owen had deemed my "science experiment," now happily frothing away in a glass container. There were also jars of wild honey, given to me by Jim, a gift of a displaced honeybee colony from a fallen tree.

I also had a basketful of figs I'd collected from a friend's backyard in Fort Greene. These figs were as large as plums, with juicy, raspberry-colored centers. Eating one directly from the tree for the first time, I thought of Hermann Hesse's description of a courtesan's mouth as being "like a freshly cut fig."

I gathered all of my wild ingredients onto my countertop and got to work.

The sesame noodle guy is done tossing his noodles, and begins plating them for the judges. He's used a secret mixture of sauces he has pulled from his kitchen pantry. The aspiring salmon caterer next to me is not impressed.

We've heard from a home cook who is beaming above her festive codfish sauté, and Rachael Mamane, whose fragrant paella, made from her own Brooklyn bouillon, I can smell from this side of the long table. The judge from the *Huffington Post* is tasting the paella, and while she's trying to maintain a neutral expression, I can tell that she likes it.

Finally, it's my turn. Someone from the neighborhood yells out "Urban Forager!" and whatever nerves I have disappear.

"This is a locally sourced tart," I say, with the dish still covered in front of me. "The main ingredients were all foraged by my own hands."

I tell the story about finding the oyster mushrooms growing high up on a tree, and clambering upon a log to collect them.

I tell them about picking figs from my friend's backyard, which is within walking distance from where we are standing.

I tell them about how the base of the tart is made from wild yeast cultivated inside my apartment.

What I leave out is the drizzle of wild honey that I've added to the tart—not because I'm not proud of the contributions of feral Staten Island bees, but because I think that this last bit might throw off the veracity of my story: wild oyster mushrooms, wild yeast, hand-plucked figs, *and wild honey?* I can hardly believe it myself.

I proceed to the unveiling. I pull away the cover, and what lies underneath is a bed of roasted oyster mushrooms and caramelized onions, the deep blush of figs, fluffy pillows of goat cheese, and a sprig of fresh rosemary—all on a thin golden pie crust that's crisped brown along the edges. The colors are so rich and sumptuous that a few onlookers in the crowd actually gasp.

"And the other ingredients are from where?" the Meatless Mondays judge asks.

"They're organic from the food coop," I say.

It's time to serve the judges. Cutting into the tart without ruining the effect is the difficult thing—the base is actually a homemade pizza dough, which lends a nice chewiness to the entire dish but doesn't cut very easily with my knife.

While the judges sample my tart, I straighten up the pan, too nervous to look. A whole half of the pie remains. Finally, the judges move on to the wannabe caterer with the salmon dish.

It starts to rain so hard that I am getting wet even under my umbrella, and I'm wondering how my pizza crust is holding up under all of this moisture. Owen leans over and takes a few photographs while the aspiring chef talks about why she chose salmon and how she hopes to launch her catering company. Several onlookers regard my tart with longing.

Then, the tasting is over and the judges are conferring together, under their umbrellas. Second place is a round of drinks for the winner and ten of his or her friends at a local bar. First place is dinner for two at a supper club.

Owen leans over and hugs me.

The heavy rain prompts us to move to the cover of the buildings, including the judges, who are standing under a tax preparation center's awning.

After several minutes of whispering and nodding, the judges turn to the small crowd of us still braving the elements.

The *Huffington Post* writer announces the third-place winner.

When she hears her name, the aspiring caterer looks up, slightly disappointed. She forces a smile and gives a quick wave. I'm listening so intently for the names that I miss what her prize is, but there's no time to ask, as they're on to the next winner.

"Second place goes to—" says the *HuffPo* judge, pausing for what seems like an ungodly length of time, "—Rachael Mamane of Brooklyn Bouillon, for her wonderful paella!"

I look at Owen, who is watching Rachael shake hands with all of the judges.

"And the first place prize goes to—" the judge says, smiling as she looks directly at me, "—our very own Urban Forager, who climbed a tree to get her ingredients!"

The judges and onlookers are suddenly clapping, and behind me someone starts hooting.

I am jumping up and down, smiling even as the rain falls around us. I feel so lucky to have found the oyster mushrooms, the figs, the wild yeast, and the gift of the honey in the first place, and that everything came together—under the right timing, in balance with nature—in the form of a delicious seasonal tart, a *winning* tart, just seems like so much good fortune that I can barely contain myself. I shake hands with the *HuffPo* judge, the Meatless Mondays guy, the baker, even the rep from the city council office. As I do so, several onlookers clap me on the back.

When the organizer announces the close of the Good Food Fest, everyone breaks out into applause and folks start to disassemble.

"Can I have a piece?" asks a resident onlooker. "And one for my friend, too?"

"Sure," I say, cutting two slices.

By the time I've finished wrapping up my equipment, all of the oyster mushroom tart has disappeared.

After dinner, Owen and I return to my neighborhood. We walk arm in arm down the western edges of the park, stepping over puddles. I cannot stop smiling.

"I really, really, really wanted to win," I say, swinging my bag full of baking equipment in my other hand. "I know you're not supposed to ever want to win—it's all about the process, the journey, what you've learned, et cetera, et cetera—but I *really* wanted to win."

It's getting dark, and up ahead, I can see the old-fashioned street lamps glowing along my block, the same lights that illuminated it the night of our first date. We've been together nearly a year, and it's taken this long for me to feel safe enough to finally admit that Owen is my boyfriend.

"You know, this is serious for me," Owen says, taking my hand as we approach my brownstone. "It isn't just another relationship."

I look at him. The lamplight illuminates his hair, so light that I can almost see through it to the sycamore above him.

"When is our anniversary—early October?"

It's coming in a few weeks, around the time of the harvest moon, during Sukkot and the Chinese Moon festival—when observant Jews around the city will be building huts and shaking palm branches, and Chinese families will be purchasing mooncakes with double egg yolks.

"Would you like to come with me to pick out something round and shiny that weekend? Or would you rather I do it and be surprised?"

I jump up and hug him—*of course I want to come and help pick it out!*—nearly tackling him as he's got his hands full of me and my baking supplies.

In a few weeks, Owen will serve his wife in Germany her divorce papers, and we will giddily visit Tiffany's and the Diamond District on 47th Street to pick out a stone as clear as water. The saleswoman who measures my ring finger will declare that it's a "four"—the same size as my grandmother's. Later, I'll begin preparing for my move to Owen's Upper East Side apartment, packing up my botanical guides and herb books, my containers full of dried mushrooms and wild yeast, and my jars of Staten Island honey. We'll merge our dishware, our books, our CDs and DVDs, and I'll attempt to squeeze all of my jars of dried motherwort and reishi mushrooms into the pantry. The dandelion roots that I've placed on our kitchen windowsill in a flowerpot for the sole purpose of forcing will spontaneously sprout in the middle of one of the coldest winters on record. We'll be eating tender young dandelion shoots while the entire city is covered under a blanket of snow.

But for now, right now, we are walking up the steps of my stoop on Twelfth Street, enjoying a warm late-summer breeze in Brooklyn, days before the chill of autumn sets in.

Owen suddenly stops and squeezes my hand. "You are my life," he says.

I open the door with my key and we enter the hallway. I've finally found a love that feels real—one of which my grandmother would have approved. I'm unexpectedly filled with the kind of relief and comfort that I normally experience only when I'm in the middle of my deepest foraging forays. As we climb the four flights of stairs to my apartment, which suddenly feels temporary, I'm certain of one thing that won't change. Whether I am in Flushing or Brooklyn or the swankiest neighborhoods in Manhattan, my life is no one else's but my own. All of these seasons of foraging have taught me that.

Once, long before my grandmother's collapse, I asked her what kind of partner she saw me with. We were sitting on the love seat in her living room in Flushing, the television on low in the background. I had been in the process of asking many of my oldest friends the same question. They'd all answered something along the lines of "smart," "creative," "stable," and "older."

My grandmother considered it a moment, looking thoughtfully from behind her glasses.

"I think women need a lot of love," she said, "especially you, who didn't have a father."

She paused. "He should be really loving. As long as he loves you, that's all that matters."

At the time it felt like the most frustrating answer that I had ever received. I had to admit that I needed love? It seemed so simple, so antifeminist.

I don't need love. I don't need a man. I can do things for myself, I thought, *just like my mother.*

When I returned home, I realized that I wasn't sure how to recognize "loving." It wasn't something you could tick off a box for, like "college-educated" or "financially secure" or "home-owner." It wasn't even readily apparent, like "funny," "gregarious," "laid-back," or even "quiet." How would I be able to see such an elusive quality?

It was only after she died that I fully realized that my grandmother was saying what she wanted for me: *You should be with someone who really loves you. Someone who will love you like I do, even after I'm gone.*

Urban Forager Wild Oyster Mushroom, Fig, & Goat Cheese Tart with Caramelized Onions

It may sound unusual at first, but this unlikely combination of flavors produces one of the yummiest tarts I've ever tasted. All of the wild foods can be substituted by items found in farmers' markets or grocery stores, although I prefer locally grown or harvested ingredients, as you may have guessed. Use the freshest oyster mushrooms, figs, and goat cheese you can find, and try your hand at making your own wild yeast starter—it yields a zingier, more flavorful crust.

The first time I made this, I enjoyed reading up on wild yeast pizza dough–making from the Pizza Goon, John Gutekanst, an award-winning pizza maker and owner of Avalanche Pizza Bakers in Athens, Ohio. You can find his recipes and videos on his blog (PizzaGoon.com). My own Brooklyn-mother experiences, and a recipe for how to make a wild yeast starter, can be found here: www.AvaChin.com and cityroom.blogs.nytimes .com/2010/10/16/urban-forager-free-roaming-yeast-brooklyn -bred/. The pie dough should be made a day in advance.

Please note, wild yeast takes longer to rise than store-bought varieties but yields a greater, more sourdough-like flavor. The instructions for allowing the dough to rest outside the refrigerator are to enable that natural rise.

For Pie Dough

1 cup wild yeast starter (left out at room temperature at least 4 hours, but preferably overnight)

1 cup organic bread flour

1 teaspoon salt

1 teaspoon extra virgin olive oil

Oiled parchment paper to fit 9-inch pan

For Tart

1 teaspoon extra virgin olive oil or butter

$1/2$ pound oyster mushrooms, sliced

$1/2$ teaspoon salt and pepper, retaining pinch of salt for onions and crust

1 medium onion, sliced thinly

$1/2$ teaspoon Dijon mustard

5 medium figs, sliced in half or thirds

4 ounces goat cheese

$1/2$ teaspoon rosemary, crushed, plus 1 sprig

1 teaspoon honey (if possible, use wild honey, as it's more flavorful than domesticated honey)

Pie Dough Directions

>> **Yields enough for two 9-inch pies, one to serve, another to keep on reserve**

1. Mix the yeast starter with the flour by hand, creating a ball. Add the salt and extra virgin olive oil.

2. Knead the dough, folding it, until you have a nicely formed ball.

3. Cover with a clean cloth and let rest for 1 hour in a bowl.

4. Place in refrigerator for 4 hours.

5. Allow the dough to return to room temperature, rising overnight. Use right away or store in the freezer in plastic wrap for up to 3 months.

Tart Directions

1. Roll out the dough into a 9-inch pie pan and flatten. Cover with oiled parchment paper and replace in the refrigerator until ready to bake. Preheat the oven to 300 °F.

2. Brush the oven tray with the extra virgin olive oil and lay out the mushrooms. Sprinkle with the salt and pepper.

3. Roast the mushrooms for about 7 minutes on each side, or until browned. Set aside.

4. Sauté the onions over medium heat with a pinch of salt, stirring frequently, until caramelized (this can take upwards of half an hour). Lower heat, if necessary.

5. Raise the oven temperature to 450 °F. Remove flattened pie dough from refrigerator. Brush on a light coating of Dijon mustard; add the caramelized onions, roasted mushrooms, and fig slices to the tart. Add small dollops of goat cheese intermittently throughout the dish.

6. Sprinkle the rosemary around the entire pie. Add a swirling drizzle of wild honey. Add a bit of salt along the edges of the piecrust. Top off with the sprig of fresh rosemary in the center.

7. Bake for 25 minutes, or until crust is golden. Cool tart in pan on rack. Let stand at room temperature before serving.

Acknowledgments

This book couldn't have been written without the help of so many wonderful friends and readers. Thank you, Lydie Raschka, Carlos Hernandez, John Cohoon, Kathleen McGraw, and Mara Faye Lethem for your keen insight and valuable editing eyes. Also, to everyone at the Library and the members of the Memoir Writers' groups—you know who you are—especially librarians Carolyn Waters and Patrick Rayner, for all of their help.

Thanks to my editors and writer friends, including Andy Newman, Mary Ann Giordano, Indrani Sen, Tracie McMillan, Karen Cook, and Betsy Carter. To Elisabeth Vincentelli, Robyn Sunderland, and the entire Vincentelli family for the inspiring grass pie.

Special shout-outs are due to the foragers near and far who guided me along the way, including Daniel Glaser, Jim Brochu (aka Puma Ghostwalker), Deborah Kaufmann, Brigitte Mars, and the "Wildman" Steve Brill. Also, to members of the New York Mycological Society, including Gary Lincoff, Paul Sadowski, Dennis Aita, Jason Cortlund, Eugenia Bone, Arlene Jacobs, Victor Weiss, Claudine Michaud, Anne Yen, and the late Bill Parsons.

Experts at the Brooklyn Botanic Gardens helped in plant identification and in other ways too many to list. Thank you most especially Elizabeth Scholtz, Caleb Leech, Paul Harwood, Uli Lorimer, Barbara Kurland, and Adele Rossetti Morosini.

A very special thank-you to my stellar agent, Melissa Flashman at Trident Media, who helped with the manuscript from draft proposal to finished product. And special thanks to Emily Graff, Karyn Marcus, Karen Thompson, Nick Greene, and the entire Simon & Schuster editorial team, including the publicity and marketing departments.

Also to the communities of Fort Greene and Clinton Hill, Brooklyn, and the residents and friends who welcomed me into their backyards, front yards, and onto their stoops, especially Heidi Chua, Emily Wasserman, Andrew Hsiao, and Don Palmer.

Lastly, thank you to my family, especially Owen and our daughter, Mei Rose. Every day with you reminds me that the world is rich in bountiful gifts.

REFERENCES

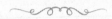

Soil testing can often be done inexpensively through your local college agricultural extension office. Brooklyn College and Cornell University, for example, offer affordable testing.

Environmental Sciences Analytical Center
Department of Earth and Environmental Sciences
Brooklyn College
5135 Ingersoll Hall
2900 Bedford Avenue
Brooklyn, NY 11210
www.brooklyn.cuny.edu/web/academics/centers/esac/services
/soil.php

Cornell Nutrient Analysis Laboratory (CNAL)
G01 Bradfield Hall
Cornell University
Ithaca, NY 14853-1901
(607) 255-4540
http://soilhealth.cals.cornell.edu/

Flora

Allen, David E., and Gabrielle Hatfield. *Medicinal Plants in Folk Tradition: An Ethnobotany of Britain & Ireland*. Portland, OR: Timber Press, 2004.
Bracket, Babette, and Maryann Lash. *The Wild Gourmet: a Forager's Cookbook*. Boston, MA: D. R. Godine, 1975.

Brill, Steve. *Identifying and Harvesting Edible and Medicinal Plants.* New York, NY: HarperCollins, 1994.

Bubel, Mike, and Nancy Bubel. *Root Cellaring: Natural Cold Storage of Roots and Vegetables.* North Adams, MA: Storey Publishing, 1991.

Coyle, Meaghan, Caroline Smith, and Brian Peat. 2005. "Cephalic version by moxibustion for breech presentation." *Cochrane Database of Systematic Reviews* (5): CD003928.

Datta, R. K. *Global Silk Industry: A Complete Source Book.* New Delhi: APH Publishing, 2007.

Del Tredici, Peter. *Wild Urban Plants of the Northeast: A Field Guide.* Ithaca, NY: Cornell University Press, 2010.

Elias, Thomas, and Peter Dykeman. *Edible Wild Plants: A North American Field Guide to Over 200 Natural Foods.* New York, NY: Sterling, 2009.

Foster, Steven, and James Duke. *Peterson Field Guides Eastern/Central Medicinal Plants and Herbs.* Boston, MA: Houghton Mifflin, 2000.

Gibbons, Euell. *Stalking the Wild Asparagus, Field Guide Edition.* New York: David Mackey Company, 1970.

———. *Stalking the Healthful Herbs.* Brattleboro, VT: Alan C. Hood, 1989.

Hoffman, David. *The Herbal Handbook.* Rochester, VT: Healing Arts Press, 1998.

Kindscher, Kelly. *Edible Wild Plants of the Prairie: An Ethnobotanical Guide.* Lawrence, KS: University Press of Kansas, 1987.

Mabey, Richard. *Food for Free: A Guide to the Edible Wild Plants of Britain.* London: William Collins Sons, 1973.

———. *Weeds: In Defense of Nature's Most Unloved Plants.* New York, NY: HarperCollins, 2010.

Moerman, Daniel E. *Native American Medicinal Plants: An Ethnobotanical Dictionary.* Portland, OR: Timber Press, 2009.

National Park Service, Plant Conservation Alliance's Alien Plant Working Group, www.nps.gov/plants/alien/fact/alpe1.htm.

Peterson, Lee Allen. *Peterson Field Guides Edible Wild Plants: Eastern/Central North America.* Boston, MA: Houghton Mifflin, 1977.

Peterson, Roger Tory, and Margaret McKenny. *Peterson Field Guides Wildflowers: Northeastern and North-central North America.* Boston, MA: Houghton Mifflin, 1968.

Pond, Barbara. *A Sampler of Wayside Herbs: Rediscovering Old Uses for Familiar Wild Plants.* New York, NY: The Chatham Press, 1974.

Seebeck, Cattail Bob. *Best-Tasting Wild Plants of Colorado and the Rockies.* Boulder, CO: Westcliffe Publishers, 1998.

Swearingen, J., K. Reshetiloff, B. Slattery, and S. Zwicker. *Plant Invaders of Mid-Atlantic Natural Areas.* National Park Service and U.S. Fish & Wildlife Service, 2002. www.invasive.org/eastern/midatlantic/hefu.html.

USDA Plants Profile website: plants.usda.gov/java/profile?symbol=alvi.

Willard, Terry. *Edible and Medicinal Plants of the Rocky Mountains and Neighboring Territories*. Calgary: Wild Rose College, 1992.

Fungi

Arora, David. *Mushrooms Demystified*. Berkeley, CA: Ten Speed Press, 1986.

Bone, Eugenia. *Mycophilia: Revelations from the Weird World of Mushrooms*. New York: Rodale Books, 2011.

Kuo, Michael. www.MushroomExpert.com.

Lincoff, Gary. *National Audubon Society Field Guide to North American Mushrooms*. New York, NY: Knopf, 1981.

———. *The Complete Mushroom Hunter: An Illustrated Guide to Finding, Harvesting, and Enjoying Wild Mushrooms*. Beverly, MA: Quarry Books, 2010.

Miller, Orson. *Mushrooms of North America*. New York, NY: Plume, 1977.

Missouri Department of Conservation Online. mdc.mo.gov/discover-nature /field-guide.

Schmitt, C., and M. Tatum. "Malheur National Forest: Location of the World's Largest Organism [The Humongous Fungus]." USDA, 2008.

Volk, Tom. *Fungus of the Month* website, University of Wisconsin. botit .botany.wisc.edu/toms_fungi/aug99.html; botit.botany.wisc.edu/toms_ fungi/mar2005.html.

Honeybees

"Anatomy of the Honey Bee." Cornell University Cooperative Extension. www.extension.org/pages/21754/anatomy-of-the-honey-bee.

Darwin, Charles. *The Origin of Species: By Means of Natural Selection of the Preservation of Favoured Races in the Struggle for Life*. New York, NY: Signet Classics, 2003.

Gould, James, and Carol Gould. *The Honey Bee*. New York, NY: Scientific American, 1988.

"Honey Bees Colony and Collapse Disorder." U.S. Department of Agriculture's Agricultural Research Service. www.ars.usda.gov/News/docs .htm?docid=15572#history.

"How Do Bees Make Honey?" *Lansing State Journal*. July 30, 1997. Michigan State's Science Theater archives. www.pa.msu.edu/sciencet/ask_ st/073097.html.

Kaplan, Kim. "Survey Reports Latest Honey Bee Losses." U.S. Department of Agriculture, Agricultural Research Service. April 29, 2010.

Speake, Jennifer. *Oxford Dictionary of Proverbs*, 4th ed. New York: Oxford University Press, 2003.

Food

David, Elizabeth. *English Bread & Yeast Cookery, American Edition.* New York, NY: Viking Press, 1980.

Green, Connie, and Sarah Scott. *The Wild Table: Seasonal Foraged Food and Recipes.* New York, NY: Viking Studio, 2010.

Gutekanst, John. "Pizza Margherita Using Wild Yeast Pizza Dough," pizzagoon.com/uncategorized/pizza-margherita-using-wild-yeast-pizza-dough/.

———. "Wild Yeast Pizza Levain (or Starter)," pizzagoon.com/uncategorized/wild-yeast-pizza-levain-or-starter/.

Murray, Dawn. "Ricotta Spinach Pie." *Bon Apétit,* March 1996, www.epicurious.com/recipes/food/views/Ricotta-Spinach-Pie-1548.

Pollan, Michael. *In Defense of Food: An Eater's Manifesto.* New York, NY: Penguin Books, 2009.

Wizenberg, Molly. *A Homemade Life: Stories and Recipes from My Kitchen Table.* New York, NY: Simon & Schuster, 2009.

Young, Grace. *The Wisdom of the Chinese Kitchen: Classic Family Recipes for Celebration and Healing.* New York, NY: Simon & Schuster, 1999.

Foraging Practices

Allemansrätten, The Right of Public Access, www.geonord.org/law/publ.access.html.

Lin, Joy Hui. "Sweden's Every Man's Right Is a Forager's Dream." *Saveur,* April 7, 2011.

Mabey, Richard. *Food for Free: A Guide to the Edible Wild Plants of Britain.* London: William Collins Sons, 1973.

U.K. Theft Act of 1968, www.legislation.gov.uk/ukpga/1968/60.

Wright, John. *The River Cottage Edible Seashore Handbook.* London: Bloomsbury, 2009.

Literature

Shakespeare, William. *Romeo and Juliet.* New York: Signet Classics, 1998.

Thoreau, Henry David. *The Journal: 1837–1861.* New York, NY: New York Review of Books Classics, 2009.

———. Carl Bode, ed. *The Portable Thoreau.* New York, NY: Penguin, 1982.

Parks

Graff, M. M. *Central Park/Prospect Park: A New Perspective.* New York, NY: Greensward Foundation, 1985.

Lancaster, Clay. *Prospect Park Handbook.* New York: Walton H. Rawls, 1967.

Schaffer, Julia. "Fort Greene Park." Fort Greene Park Conservancy, 2009, NYC Parks and Recreation, www.nycgovparks.org/parks/FortGreenePark.

INDEX

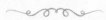

About the Author

Ava Chin, a Queens native, is the former Urban Forager columnist for the *New York Times*. She has written for the *Los Angeles Times*, *Saveur*, the *Village Voice*, and *Martha Stewart* online, and has appeared on NPR's *All Things Considered*. She holds a Ph.D. from the University of Southern California and an M.A. from the Writing Seminars at Johns Hopkins University. A professor of creative nonfiction at CUNY, she lives in New York City with her husband and daughter. For more information please visit www.avachin.com.